TEACHING THROUGH GAMES

TEACHING FINANCIAL LITERACY THROUGH PLAY

WITHDRAWN

CHRISTOPHER HARRIS AND PATRICIA HARRIS, Ph.D.

Rosen
Classroom
PROFESSIONAL RESOURCES™

Published in 2015 by The Rosen Publishing Group, Inc.
29 East 21st Street, New York, NY 10010

First Edition

Cataloging-in-Publication Data

Harris, Christopher.
Teaching financial literacy through play/by Christopher Harris and Patricia Harris, PhD.
    p. cm. — (Teaching through games)
Includes appendix.
ISBN 978-1-4994-9010-7 (paperback)
1. Children — Finance, Personal — Study and teaching. 2. Consumer education — Study and teaching. 3. Saving and investment — Study and teaching. I. Harris, Christopher, 1977-. II. Harris, Patricia. III. Title.
HG179. H37 2015
332.024—d23

Manufactured in the United States of America

Code Word: spendwell

Use the code word above to register for an account on the series website at http://teachingthroughgames.com. Or, if you have already registered, use the code to add this book to your existing account. The website contains the readings and sheets referenced in this book as well as additional game elements. There is also a discussion forum where you can share successful practices and ask questions.

Photo Credits: cover (safe), p. i © DIMDIMICH/www.istockphoto.com; cover (background) © CTRd/www.istockphoto.com; cover (arrow) pp. i, 73 © Kerem Yucel/www.istockphoto.com; pp. iv-v © Björn Meyer/www.istockphoto.com.

CONTENTS

INTRODUCTION

Teaching financial literacy through play seems almost a bit like a cliché. After all, we regularly talk about playing the ponies or playing the market. When the values on financial spreadsheets get too big to comprehend, we say it is just a numbers game. In our minds, finance and gameplay are inexorably linked. So why not make use of this powerful connection to help students understand some of the key concepts of financial literacy to better prepare them for a life of financial success?

ELEMENTS OF FINANCIAL LITERACY

In the United States, the Financial Literacy and Education Commission, established by Congress in 2003 and chaired by the secretary of the treasury, provides guidelines for teaching about finances. The commission's website at mymoney.gov lists five key elements of financial literacy:

Earn: Everyone should understand what goes into and comes out of a paycheck, including taxes, withholdings, and other deductions.

Save and Invest: Everyone should be saving money for the future in ways that can help meet short- and long-term goals while establishing a buffer for emergencies.

Protect: Precautions need to be taken to avoid financial scams.

Spend: It is OK to spend money, but everyone should understand how to develop a budget to help live within their means and avoid debt.

Borrow: Be aware of borrowing habits, including the use of credit cards, as high-interest rates and large debts can lead to financial ruin.

In addition to these personal finance elements, it is critical for students to understand how businesses work. Whether students want to pursue entrepreneurial opportunities or just have a better understanding of how investments work, knowing what goes into sound business strategies can have a positive impact on personal finances as well.

In this book, we will use games that address both personal and business finances, as well as a more abstract game that teaches about risk assessment and return on investment. The goal is to present a balanced approach that covers many aspects of financial literacy from different perspectives.

GAMES AND HIGH FINANCE

Finance has long been used as both a theme and a mechanism for board games. Familiar classics like Monopoly, PayDay, and the Game of Life all use interactions with money as a key component of the game. The financial aspects of these games were actually quite limited, though. Considered on a continuum of chance versus strategy, games like Monopoly are almost pure chance. The properties you purchase are not dictated by strategy, but rather by the roll of the dice. The only real strategic decisions are whether or not to buy the properties you land on. Spoiler alert: buy the properties.

Financial games took a huge leap forward in 1962 with the publication of Sid Sackson's Aquire as part of the 3M Book Shelf Games series. In this game, players are hotel magnates building up hotel empires through acquisition of smaller hotel chains. Widely considered to be the first modern board game, Acquire introduced a much higher level of strategy that gave players more control over their financial destiny. There is still a level of chance in the game—a common mechanism used in many games to level the playing field between experts and novices—but the choices made by players as they work toward a goal matter much more than in most games that came before.

Where earlier games had dealt almost entirely with personal finances—even in Monopoly, you are playing the role of an individual property owner making purchases on a personal level—in Acquire you are dealing with high finance. You are controlling a business and dealing with business considerations like mergers and takeovers. This opened the door to a new world for games to explore.

TRAIN GAMES

In 1974, Francis Tresham designed a game that would define an entire genre. A game about train companies in southern Britain, 1829, became the first game in what is now referred to as the 18xx style. The genre is so named because many of the games in this style are titled as the year of railroad business they are depicting similarly to 1829. Since the publication of the first 18xx game in 1974, there have been more than fifty additional titles in the same style. An impressive number considering that these are very detailed games that can take hours to play.

In these games, players are managing railroad companies within a very detailed financial world. The games typically start out with players purchasing an initial railroad company at auction that gives them some starting income and abilities. Then the major companies are formed. Players can purchase stock in any companies; the player with the most shares of stock in a company acts as the president. One player may be president of multiple companies while another player may not actually be president of any companies. The stock market aspect of the game is also very detailed, with shares going up and down in price based on the payment of dividends.

A key aspect of the games is the separation of a player's personal money from the funds of any companies he or she is managing. At the end of the game, the player with the highest personal wealth is the winner. This requires careful management of company funds with payments of dividends and measured payment of salary to the president. If a company runs out of funds and is required to make a purchase, the president may find himself or herself on the hook for paying for a new train.

PLAYING TO LEARN

In this book, we will use a game inspired by the 18xx series as a capstone exercise. Chicago Express, the game featured in chapter four, will force players to make careful decisions as they cooperate and compete with others in the game. Students will need to draw upon everything they learned in the first three games in order to be financially successful in Chicago Express. What new skills will they bring to bear in the capstone game?

In the first game, High Society, players will learn about spending and saving as they create budgets to help them be successful within this devious little auction game designed by Reiner Knizia. One of the most prolific modern game designers, Knizia has numerous games that explore different aspects of the auction mechanism. In High Society, players are bidding to buy luxury items (or avoid misfortunes) in order to increase their final score. Careful budgeting will be key to success, however, as at the end of the game the player with the least amount of money remaining will be eliminated before the game is scored. Big spending is not the path to victory in this game, or in life. Rather, cautious and measured spending within an established budget will help players win.

The second game, Sid Sackson's Can't Stop, is a classic game that explores risk assessment and return on investment using an abstract dice rolling mechanism. Each turn, players will roll dice in an attempt to keep moving forward in columns on the board based on resulting summed pairs of dice. But be careful, press your luck too far and fail to roll a sum in one of your active columns and your whole turn is lost. Players have to think very carefully about risk vs. reward. Luckily there is quite a bit of math available to help with this.

Panic on Wall Street, the third game in this book, throws students into the chaos of an open call trading floor. This game supports up to eleven players divided into teams of investors and company managers. Each team will have a winner who is the most successful at navigating the stock market to steadily increase wealth over the game. Some stocks offer massive reward but carry huge risks as well. Will players take the safe road or risk everything for a huge payout? This game, which builds upon the skills learned in Can't Stop, challenges players to think about saving and investing in the real world as well as in the game.

Finally, as noted above, the capstone game Chicago Express will let players take on the role of investors in railroad companies. Students will have to calculate budgets for the companies, evaluate risk, determine potential return on investment, and understand dividends and the stock market in order to be successful.

INSTRUCTIONAL SUPPORT

In some of the chapters, you will also find primary source documents provided as readings to support the content being discussed. These were selected as keystone documents in history—an essay by Benjamin Franklin about *Poor Richard's Almanac*, one of FDR's Fireside Chats, and a technical report about the 1987 Wall Street crash—that exemplify ways in which citizens have been informed about financial information over time. It is suggested that you use timely articles from newspapers and magazines to provide additional readings on current financial events and trends. Another excellent resource is the Financial Literacy database available through Rosen Digital.

LESSON 1:
SPENDING AND SAVING IN HIGH SOCIETY

O ne of the most important aspects of personal finance is a strong understanding of the importance of saving and the risks associated with credit and debt. Not all debt is bad, but uncontrolled spending and a lack of savings can lead to financial ruin. In Reiner Knizia's High Society (Gryphon Games, 2008) players will have to carefully manage their spending and saving. To win the game, you have to purchase items worth victory points. Be careful, though, because at the end of the game the player with the least amount of money remaining on hand is eliminated before scoring. Spend too much and you can still end up losing no matter how many points you have accumulated.

FINANCIAL LITERACY INFORMATION

SPENDING AND SAVING

This game accurately reflects the careful balance between spending and saving that is required for financial success. To be successful, players must carefully consider each expenditure in relation to their available resources. As will be seen in the lesson plans, one way to better plan for success in the game—and life—is to create a personal budget. Budgets, or spending plans, are often based around balance sheets that allow comparison between a column of assets and a column of liabilities. Assets include income, property, and available savings while liabilities represent debts or expenditures. The difference between assets and liabilities is known as equity; hopefully this is a positive number that shows more assets than liabilities. By developing a budget for High Society, players can become more comfortable with the idea of recording how they are saving and spending and the need for a detailed plan to insure financial success.

One of the risks of spending without careful planning is debt. Though High Society doesn't deal directly with issues of credit, debt, and interest fees, it does feature a mechanism that penalizes rampant spending. At the end of the game, just before scoring, the player with the least amount of money remaining in hand is eliminated. The key is to carefully balance spending and saving—avoiding overspending and debt by having a clear plan for purchasing that fits within a budget.

Budgeting

One requirement for a budget to work is delayed gratification, waiting to buy what you want to buy, saying "no" to a purchase you want, until your "needs" are met and you have enough money to afford the item. If you have a credit card, using that card to buy items for which you do not have available liquid assets means that you are incurring a debt with an interest payment, often very high, unless you pay off the card each month. Credit cards make it easy to avoid delayed gratification, but they also make it easy to spend money you don't have. Paying off a credit card debt from a previous month is often difficult for many people who then find themselves in financial difficulty.

Debit cards avoid the problem of using money one doesn't have because they require you to have the money in the account that is accessed by a merchant. ATMs work the same way. However, having ready cash in your pocket or in the form of a card that lets you access your assets in the bank immediately can also make saving and staying with a budget more difficult. It is almost too easy to spend money you have readily available when you want something that is not in your budget!

With this first game, more time is devoted to the readings and the game experiences as a way to introduce students to basic ideas and practices in financial literacy.

LESSON PLAN 1A

ESSENTIAL QUESTION

How can a budget support financial success?

VOCABULARY

The following vocabulary words are important concepts for the content in this lesson:
- Budget
- Assets
- Liability
- Delayed gratification
- Credit
- Debt

SUGGESTED READING RESOURCES

Primary Source Document:
"The Way to Wealth" by Benjamin Franklin, 1757. This document is included after the lesson in an annotated form with vocabulary underlined and some important passages for close reading highlighted; it is available online at www.teachingthroughgames.com for printing.

Other Sources
Frequently Asked Questions About Financial Literacy, pp.4-10
Written by Mary-Lane Kamberg
Published by Rosen Publishing Group, Inc., 2011
ISBN: 9781448813278

MINI READING LESSON

While you are reading the available text material or the suggested reading resources, attempt to answer the following question: What are the components of a budget? Introduce the vocabulary words above. They can be introduced even if they are not in the specific reading you have chosen.

GUIDED PRACTICE

Have students preview any headings and subheadings in the reading they have been asked to do. Have students read the selections. Review with students that if they want to create a budget for their own finances, they would need to know their total income and list all their expenses and closely track where their money has gone when they have been spending without a budget. This information could then be used to create a first budget that could be modified over time. Tell the students that as a group, they will create budgets for their life style with a fixed monthly allowance (appropriate to the average economic level of the students) that you will give them. Have them set a goal for a major purchase. Create a budget as a group. Then introduce a credit card to the group and let them use the card to "purchase" items you have gathered. Do not mention the budget or the goal. Possibly, unless students are very aware of credit card use, they will overspend their budget. After the purchases are completed, present students with a statement with 20 percent interest rate if not paid in full. Discuss the use of credit and the budget they set. Discuss the differences between credit cards and debit cards. Talk about delayed gratification. Introduce High Society as a game that requires the players to be aware of money spent and goals if they are to be winners.

Read and Discuss

Have students reread each section of the text and discuss the following:
- What is the relationship between assets and liabilities?
- Can developing a budget keep you financially sound?
- How are credit cards and debit cards alike and different?

MODEL

Play High Society without the three recognition cards and three misfortune cards shown in the manual. While groups are playing, have players talk about how they can keep track of the money others are spending. Every round, have each student total the money cards he or she has and attempt to total those the other players have. Have them check to see if the totals they gave for other players are correct or close to correct. Remind them that the poorest player at the end of the game loses. Other players win because they have the highest status points. Also remind students that no change is given in this game and so they need to stay aware of their money card distribution.

INDEPENDENT PRACTICE

Remind students of the vocabulary introduced for their reading and ask them to attempt to include that vocabulary in appropriate ways in the writing activities they do.

Writing Activities

Narrative: Write about a time when you bought an item from the game as indicated on the cards that you want most. Tell how you considered your budget and entered into a bidding war to buy the item. Decide if you paid so much that you ran out of money or if you bid for a good price you could afford.

Inform or Explain: Explain how a budget can help one reach a long-term goal.

Opinion: Is it fair to have the player with the lowest money automatically be a loser in the game? Support your opinion.

SHARING/REFLECTION

Have individuals or groups share and discuss their work with the class.

ASSESSMENT

Collect writing activities and review. During the model section check on how accurate the students are at keeping track of amounts of money spent. If needed, ask for suggestions from groups on how they could better track the spending of others. The narrative section should reflect thinking about their budget but may also reflect that the student ignored the plans set. For the inform piece, students should include points on how a budget can help and writing should reflect an understanding of long-term goals. Answers will vary in the opinion piece but support should be given for the position taken.

EXTENSION ACTIVITIES

Further Research: Write an essay on how the cost of living in different parts of the country affects budgets.

Important Details: Have students identify ten important details to know about budget and justify their choices of those details using the Important Details sheet in the appendix and available online at www.teachingthroughgames.com for printing. Answers will vary.

BENJAMIN FRANKLIN'S "THE WAY TO WEALTH"

Courteous Reader,

I have heard that nothing gives an author so great pleasure, as to find his works respectfully quoted by other learned authors. This pleasure I have seldom enjoyed; for tho' I have been, if I may say it without vanity, an <u>eminent</u> author of <u>almanacs</u> annually now a full quarter of a century, my brother authors in the same way, for what reason I know not, have ever been very sparing in their applauses; and no other author has taken the least notice of me, so that did not my writings produce me some solid pudding, the great deficiency of praise would have quite discouraged me.

I concluded at length, that the people were the best judges of my merit; for they buy my works; and besides, in my rambles, where I am not personally known, I have frequently heard one or other of my adages repeated, with, as Poor Richard says, at the end on't; this gave me some satisfaction, as it showed not only that my instructions were regarded, but discovered likewise some respect for my authority; and I own, that to encourage the practice of remembering and repeating those wise sentences, I have sometimes quoted myself with great gravity.

Judge then how much I must have been gratified by an incident I am going to relate to you. I stopped my horse lately where a great number of people were collected at a vendue of merchant goods. The hour of sale not being come, they were conversing on the badness of the times, and one of the company called to a plain clean old man, with white locks, "Pray, Father Abraham, what think you of the times? Won't these heavy taxes quite ruin the country? How shall we be ever able to pay them? What would you advise us to?" Father Abraham stood up, and replied, "If you'd have my advice, I'll give it you in short, for a word to the wise is enough, and many words won't fill a bushel, as Poor Richard says." They joined in desiring him to speak his mind, and gathering round him, he proceeded as follows:

"Friends, says he, and neighbors, the taxes are indeed very heavy, and if those laid on by the government were the only ones we had to pay, we might more easily discharge them; but we have many others, and much more grievous to some of us. **We are taxed twice as much by our idleness, three times as much by our pride, and four times as much by our folly, and from these taxes the commissioners cannot ease or deliver us by allowing an abatement.** However let us hearken to good advice, and something may be done for us; God helps them that help themselves, as Poor Richard says, in his almanac of 1733.

"It would be thought a hard government that should tax its people one tenth part of their time, to be employed in its service. But idleness taxes many of us much more, if we reckon all that is spent in absolute sloth, or doing of nothing, with that which is spent in idle employments or amusements, that amount to nothing. Sloth,by bringing on diseases, absolutely shortens life. Sloth, like rust, consumes faster than labor wears, while the used key is always bright, as Poor Richard says. But dost thou love life, then do not squander time, for that's the stuff life is made of, as Poor Richard says. How much more than is necessary do we spend in sleep! forgetting that the sleeping fox catches no poultry, and that there will be sleeping enough in the grave, as Poor Richard says. If time be of all things the most precious, wasting time must be, as Poor Richard says, the greatest prodigality, since, as he elsewhere tells us, lost time is never found again, and what we call time-enough, always proves little enough: let us then be up and be doing, and doing to the purpose; so by diligence shall we do more with less perplexity. Sloth makes all things difficult, but industry all easy, as Poor Richard says; and he that riseth late, must trot all day, and shall scarce overtake his business at night. While laziness travels so slowly, that poverty soon overtakes him, as we read in Poor Richard, who adds, drive thy business, let not that drive thee; and early to bed, and early to rise, makes a man healthy, wealthy and wise.

"So what signifies wishing and hoping for better times. We may make these times better if we bestir ourselves. Industry need not wish, as Poor Richard says, and he that lives upon hope will die fasting. There are no gains, without pains, then help hands, for I have no lands, or if I have, they are smartly taxed. And, as **Poor Richard likewise observes, he that hath a trade hath an estate, and he that hath a calling hath an office of profit and honor; but then the trade must be worked at, and the calling well followed, or neither the estate, nor the office, will enable us to pay our taxes.** If we are industrious we shall never starve; for, as Poor Richard says, at the working man's house hunger looks in, but dares not enter. Nor will the bailiff nor the constable enter, for industry pays debts, while despair encreaseth them, says Poor Richard. What though you have found no treasure, nor has any rich relation left you a legacy, diligence is the mother of good luck, as Poor Richard says, and God gives all things to industry. Then plough deep, while sluggards sleep, and you shall have corn to sell and to keep, says Poor Dick. Work while it is called today, for you know not how much you may be hindered tomorrow, which makes Poor Richard say, one today is worth two tomorrows; and farther, have you somewhat to do tomorrow, do it today. If you were a servant, would you not be ashamed that a good master should catch you idle? Are you then your own master, be ashamed to catch yourself idle, as Poor Dick says. When there is so much to be done for yourself, your family, your country, and your gracious king, be up by peep of day; let not the sun look down and say, inglorious here he lies. Handle your tools without mittens; remember that the cat in gloves catches no mice, as Poor Richard says. 'Tis true there is much to be done, and perhaps you are weak handed, but stick to it steadily, and you will see great effects, for constant dropping wears away stones, and by diligence and patience the mouse ate in two the cable; and little strokes fell great oaks, as Poor Richard says in his almanac, the year I cannot just now remember.

"Methinks I hear some of you say, must a man afford himself no leisure? I will tell thee, my friend, what Poor Richard says, employ thy time well if thou meanest to gain leisure; and, since thou art not sure of a minute, throw not away an hour. Leisure is time for doing something useful; this leisure the diligent man will obtain, but the lazy man never; so that, as Poor Richard says, a life of leisure and a life of laziness are two things. Do you imagine that sloth will afford you more comfort than labor? No, for as Poor Richard says, trouble springs from idleness, and grievous toil from needless ease. Many without labor would live by their wits only, but they break for want of stock. Whereas industry gives comfort, and plenty, and respect: fly pleasures, and they'll follow you. The diligent spinner has a large shift, and now I have a sheep and a cow, everybody bids me good morrow, all which is well said by Poor Richard.

"But with our industry, we must likewise be steady, settled and careful, and oversee our own affairs with our own eyes, and not trust too much to others; for, as Poor Richard says,

I never saw an oft removed tree,
Nor yet an oft removed family,

That throve so well as those that settled be.

"And again, three removes is as bad as a fire, and again, keep the shop, and thy shop will keep thee; and again, if you would have your business done, go; if not, send. And again,

He that by the plough would thrive,
Himself must either hold or drive.

"And again, the eye of a master will do more work than both his hands; and again, want of care does us more damage than want of knowledge; and again, not to oversee workmen is to leave them your purse open. Trusting too much to others' care is the ruin of many; for, as the almanac says, in the affairs of this world men are saved not by faith, but by the want of it; but a man's own care is profitable; for, saith Poor Dick, learning is to the studious, and riches to the careful, as well as power to the bold, and Heaven to the virtuous. And farther, if you would have a faithful servant, and one that you like, serve yourself. And again, he adviseth to <u>circumspection</u> and care, even in the smallest matters, because sometimes a little neglect may breed great mischief; adding, for want of a nail the shoe was lost; for want of a shoe the horse was lost, and for want of a horse the rider was lost, being overtaken and slain by the enemy, all for want of care about a horse-shoe nail.

"So much for industry, my friends, and attention to one's own business; but to these we must add frugality, if we would make our industry more certainly successful. A man may, if he knows not how to save as he gets, keep his nose all his life to the grindstone, and die not worth a groat at last. A fat kitchen makes a lean will, as Poor Richard says; and,

Many estates are spent in the getting,
Since women for tea forsook spinning and knitting,
And men for punch forsook hewing and splitting.

If you would be wealthy, says he, in another almanac, think of saving as well as of getting: the Indies have not made Spain rich, because her outgoes are greater than her incomes. Away then with your expensive follies, and you will not have so much cause to complain of hard times, heavy taxes, and chargeable families; for, as Poor Dick says,

Women and wine, game and deceit,
Make the wealth small, and the wants great.

And farther, what maintains one vice, would bring up two children. You may think perhaps that a little tea, or a little punch now and then, diet a little more costly, clothes a little finer, and a little entertainment now and then, can be no great Matter; but remember what Poor Richard says, many a little makes a mickle, and farther, beware of little expenses; a small leak will sink a great ship, and again, who dainties love, shall beggars prove, and moreover, fools make Feasts, and wise men eat them.

"Here you are all got together at this vendue of fineries and knick-nacks. You call them goods, but if you do not take care, they will prove evils to some of you. You expect they will be sold cheap, and perhaps they may for less than they cost; but if you have no occasion for them, they must be dear to you. **Remember what Poor Richard says, buy what thou hast no need of, and ere long thou shalt sell thy necessaries.** And again, at a great pennyworth pause a while: he means, that perhaps the cheapness is apparent only, and not real; or the bargain, by straitning thee in thy business, may do thee more harm than good. **For in another place he says, many have been ruined by buying good pennyworths. Again, Poor Richard says, 'tis foolish to lay our money in a purchase of repentance; and yet this folly is practised every day at vendues, for want of minding the almanac.** Wise men, as Poor Dick says, learn by others' harms, fools scarcely by their own, but, felix quem faciunt aliena pericula cautum. Many a one, for the sake of finery on the back, have gone with a hungry belly, and half starved their families; silks and satins, scarlet and velvets, as Poor Richard says, put out the kitchen fire. These are not the necessaries of life; they can scarcely be called the conveniencies, and yet only because they look pretty, how many want to have them. The artificial wants of mankind thus become more numerous than the natural; and, as Poor Dick says, for one poor person, there are an hundred indigent. **By these, and other** <u>extravagancies</u>**, the genteel are reduced to poverty, and forced to borrow of those whom they formerly despised, but who through industry and frugality have maintained their standing; in which case it appears plainly, that a** ploughman on his legs is higher than a gentleman on his knees, as Poor Richard says. Perhaps they have had a small estate left them, which they knew not the getting of; **they think 'tis day, and will never be night; that a little to be spent out of so much, is not worth minding; (a child and a fool, as Poor Richard says, imagine twenty shillings and twenty years can never be spent) but, always taking out of the meal-tub, and never putting in, soon comes to the bottom; then, as Poor Dick says, when the well's dry, they know the worth of water.** But this they might have known before, if they had taken his advice; if you would know the value of money, go and try to borrow some, for, **he that goes a borrowing goes a sorrowing, and indeed so does he that lends to such people,** when he goes to get it in again. Poor Dick farther advises, and says,

Fond pride of dress, is sure a very curse;
E'er fancy you consult, consult your purse.

And again, pride is as loud a beggar as want, and a great deal more saucy. When you have bought one fine thing you must buy ten more, that your appearance maybe all of a piece; but Poor Dick says, 'tis easier to suppress the first desire than to satisfy all that follow it. And 'tis as truly folly for the poor to ape the rich, as for the frog to swell, in order to equal the ox.

Great estates may venture more,
But little boats should keep near shore.

'Tis however a folly soon punished; for pride that dines on vanity sups on contempt, as Poor Richard says. And in another place, pride breakfasted with plenty, dined with poverty, and supped with infamy. **And after all, of what use is this pride of appearance, for which so much is risked, so much is suffered? It cannot promote health; or ease pain; it makes no increase of merit in the person, it creates envy, it hastens misfortune.**

What is a butterfly? At best
He's but a caterpillar dressed.
The gaudy fop's his picture just,
as Poor Richard says.

"But what madness must it be to run in debt for these superfluities! We are offered, by the terms of this vendue, six months' credit; and that perhaps has induced some of us to attend it, because we cannot spare the ready money, and hope now to be fine without it. But, ah, think what you do when you run in debt; you give to another power over your liberty. If you cannot pay at the time, you will be ashamed to see your creditor; you will be in fear when you speak to him, you will make poor pitiful sneaking excuses, and by degrees come to lose you veracity, and sink into base downright lying; for, as Poor Richard says, **the second vice is lying, the first is running in debt.** And again to the same purpose, lying rides upon debt's back. Whereas a freeborn Englishman ought not to be ashamed or afraid to see or speak to any man living. But poverty often deprives a man of all spirit and virtue: 'tis hard for an empty bag to stand upright, as Poor Richard truly says. What would you think of that Prince, or that government, who should issue an edict forbidding you to dress like a gentleman or a gentlewoman, on pain of imprisonment or servitude? Would you not say, that you are free, have a right to dress as you please, and that such an edict would be a breach of your privileges, and such a government tyrannical? And yet you are about to put yourself under that tyranny when you run in debt for such dress! **Your creditor has authority at his pleasure to deprive you of your liberty, by confining you in gaol for life, or to sell you for a servant, if you should not be able to pay him! When you have got your bargain, you may, perhaps, think little of payment; but creditors, Poor Richard tells us, have better memories than debtors, and in another place says, creditors are a superstitious sect, great observers of set days and times.** The day comes round before you are aware, and the demand is made before you are prepared to satisfy it. **Or if you bear your debt in mind, the term which at first seemed so long, will, as it lessens, appear extreamly short. Time will seem to have added wings to his heels as well as shoulders. Those have a short Lent, saith Poor Richard, who owe money to be paid at Easter. Then since, as he says, the borrower is a slave to the lender, and the debtor to the creditor, disdain the chain, preserve your freedom; and maintain your independency: be**

industrious and free; be <u>frugal</u> and free. At present, perhaps, you may think yourself in thriving circumstances, and that you can bear a little extravagance without injury; but,

For age and want, save while you may;

No morning sun lasts a whole day,

as Poor Richard says. Gain may be temporary and uncertain, but ever while you live, expense is constant and certain; and 'tis easier to build two chimneys than to keep one in fuel, as Poor Richard says. So rather go to bed supperless than rise in debt.

Get what you can, and what you get hold;

'Tis the stone that will turn all your lead into gold,

as Poor Richard says. And when you have got the philosopher's stone, sure you will no longer complain of bad times, or the difficulty of paying taxes.

"This doctrine, my friends, is reason and wisdom; but after all, do not depend too much upon your own industry, and frugality, and prudence, though excellent things, for they may all be blasted without the blessing of heaven; and therefore ask that blessing humbly, and be not uncharitable to those that at present seem to want it, but comfort and help them. Remember Job suffered, and was afterwards prosperous.

"And now to conclude, experience keeps a dear school, but fools will learn in no other, and scarce in that, for it is true, we may give advice, but we cannot give conduct, as Poor Richard says: however, **remember this, they that won't be counseled, can't be helped, as Poor Richard says: and farther, that if you will not hear reason, she'll surely rap your knuckles."**

Thus the old gentleman ended his harangue. **The people heard it, and approved the doctrine, and immediately practiced the contrary, just as if it had been a common sermon; for the vendue opened, and they began to buy extravagantly, notwithstanding all his cautions, and their own fear of taxes.** I found the good man had thoroughly studied my almanacs, and digested all I had dropped on those topics during the course of five-and-twenty years. The frequent mention he made of me must have tired any one else, but my vanity was wonderfully delighted with it, though I was conscious that not a tenth part of the wisdom was my own which he ascribed to me, but rather the glean-ings I had made of the sense of all ages and nations. **However, I resolved to be the better for the echo of it; and though I had at first deter-mined to buy stuff for a new coat, I went away resolved to wear my old one a little longer. Reader, if thou wilt do the same, thy profit will be as great as mine. I am, as ever, thine to serve thee,**

Richard Saunders.
July 7, 1757.

LESSON PLAN 1B

Essential Question

How do "big spenders" and chance impact the play in High Society?

Vocabulary

The following vocabulary words are important concepts for the con-tent about financial literacy:
- High spender
- misfortune
- Luxury
- Bidding
- Wants
- Needs

Suggested Reading Resources

Primary Source Document:
"Fireside Chat 1: On the Banking Crisis." Franklin Delano Roosevelt, 1933. This document is included after the lesson in an annotated form with vocabulary underlined and some important passages for close reading highlighted; it is available online at www.teachingthroughgames.com for printing.

Other Sources:

Frequently Asked Questions About Financial Literacy
Written by Mary-Lane Kamberg
Published by Rosen Publishing Group, Inc., 2011
ISBN: 9781448813278

Top 10 Secrets for Making Money and Even More Money
Written by Maria DaSilva-Gordon
Published by Rosen Publishing Group, Inc., 2014
ISBN: 9781448893737

Mini Reading Lesson

While you are reading the available text material or the suggested reading resources, attempt to answer the following question: Why is it important to include chance misfortunes in your budget? Introduce the vocabulary words on the previous page. They can be introduced even if they are not in the specific reading you have chosen.

Guided Practice

Have students preview any headings and subheadings in the reading they have been asked to do. Have students read the selections.

Read and Discuss

Have students reread each section of the text and discuss the following:
- How do banks work? What happens with your money?
- How does a high spender in High Society differ from a high spender in your peer group? How are they alike?
- Are wants and needs defined alike by everyone? Why or why not?
- What defines luxury?
- What are some strategies for success in an auction? How can you avoid a bidding war?

MODEL

Review the rules of High Society and the mechanism for bidding within the game. The designer, Reiner Knizia, is known for his auction games, and he designed a clever and ruthless style for this game. The most notable feature is that bidders cannot take back money cards to make change. How does this impact bidding strategies? Be sure students understand that when all players have a common set of money cards, selecting the best card to bid is critical. The low cards become more valuable for their ability to make a small increase in a total bid during the late game. Players that use up all of their lower cards early will be forced to make major jumps in the bidding to counter another player's small increase. Students must also remember that bidding can go around the group multiple times. Staying within a budget can be difficult but important. It might be better to pass on a nice luxury card so that you have more money available to bid on a multiplier card or to protect yourself from a misfortune. In the heat of the moment, as players get wrapped up in a bidding war, adhering to a budget is especially hard. This is good practice for life!

INDEPENDENT PRACTICE

Have students play the game again using all of the cards and their newfound understanding of budgeting. Before playing, have students create a budget that shows how much they plan on spending for each of the possible luxury cards and special cards. Budgets should also project an ending balance that players think will be enough to keep them from being eliminated as the player with the least amount of money at the end of the game. This budget will need to remain dynamic throughout the game as some of the cards will not be included. If they purchase a luxury, they will need to record the expenditure next to the budgeted amount and then reconcile the budget by changing other elements. The best way to do this is in a spreadsheet if students are able to have mobile access to technology. The player who is eliminated for having the least amount of money at the end of the game must write an explanation as to why he or she did not budget successfully for the game. The remaining players need to write an explanation of their successful strategies for staying within their budgets while still gathering luxuries for points. If they were not the winner with the highest number of points, they should include reasons and possible changes for future successes.

Writing Activities

Remind students of the vocabulary introduced for their reading and ask them to attempt to include that vocabulary in appropriate ways in the writing activities they do.

Narrative: You just posted on Facebook about an impulse purchase. Write a series of at least ten comments including responses from your parents and peers. Your parents might be worried about your impulse purchase and lack of budgeting commitment. Your peers might be more focused on the purchase.

Inform or Explain: Explain how the mechanism of not being able to take cards away from your bid or make change for a bid causes the auction to be different from more usual auctions.

Express an Opinion: Should the element of chance in the form of recognition cards and misfortune cards exist in the game? Why or why not?

SHARING/REFLECTION

Have individuals or groups share and discuss their work with the class. It might be especially interesting to compare some successful and unsuccessful budgets from the game play.

ASSESSMENT

Collect completed formative assessment (activity for model section) and writing activities and review. In the write-ups from the game play session, students should demonstrate clear understanding of the purpose of a budget and be able to identify specific points that were successful or unsuccessful during game play. In the narrative piece, students will hopefully be able to internalize and reflect on why their parents would be pushing for commitment to a budget. The opinion pieces might express dislike of the misfortune cards but should also recognize that they are a valid representation of things that can happen in life and a reason to include emergency funds within a budget.

EXTENSION ACTIVITIES

Further Research: Research impulse buying and the marketing that goes in to trying to convince us to buy things we don't really need. Present your findings as a poster for sharing with the rest of the class.

Further Research: Create a budget for yourself. Be sure to consider sources of income and the need for long-term savings as well as the importance of having some money for fun.

PRESIDENT ROOSEVELT, FIRESIDE CHAT 1: ON THE BANKING CRISIS

March 12, 1933.

I want to talk for a few minutes with the people of the United States about banking—with the comparatively few who understand the mechanics of banking but more particularly with the overwhelming majority who use banks for the making of deposits and the drawing of checks. I want to tell you what has been done in the last few days, why it was done, and what the next steps are going to be. **I recognize that the many proclamations from state capitols and from Washington, the legislation, the treasury regulations, etc., couched for the most part in banking and legal terms should be explained for the benefit of the average citizen.** I owe this in particular because of the fortitude and good temper with which everybody has accepted the inconvenience and hardships of the banking holiday. **I know that when you understand what we in Washington have been about I shall continue to have your** cooperation as fully as I have had your sympathy and help during the past week.

First of all let me state the simple fact that **when you deposit money in a bank the bank does not put the money into a safe deposit vault. It invests your money in many different forms of credit—bonds, commercial paper, mortgages and many other kinds of loans.** In other words, the bank puts your money to work to keep the wheels of industry and of agriculture turning around. A comparatively small part of the money you put into the bank is kept in currency—an amount which in normal times is wholly sufficient to cover the cash needs of the average citizen. In other words, the total amount of all the currency in the country is only a small fraction of the total deposits in all of the banks.

What, then, happened during the last few days of February and the first few days of March? **Because of undermined confidence on the part of the public, there was a general rush by a large portion of our population to turn bank deposits into currency or gold—a rush so great that the soundest banks could not get enough currency to meet the demand.** The reason for this was that on the spur of the moment it was, of course, impossible to sell perfectly sound assets of a bank and convert them into cash except at panic prices far below their real value.

By the afternoon of March 3d scarcely a bank in the country was open to do business. <u>Proclamations</u> temporarily closing them in whole or in part had been issued by the governors in almost all the states.

It was then that I issued the proclamation providing for the nation-wide bank holiday, and this was the first step in the government's reconstruction of our financial and economic fabric.

The second step was the legislation promptly and patriotically passed by the Congress confirming my proclamation and broadening my powers so that it became possible in view of the requirement of time to extend the holiday and lift the ban of that holiday gradually. This law also gave authority to develop a program of <u>rehabilitation</u> of our banking facilities. **I want to tell our citizens in every part of the nation that the national Congress — Republicans and Democrats alike — showed by this action a devotion to public welfare and a realization of the emergency and the necessity for speed that it is difficult to match in our history.**

The third stage has been the series of regulations permitting the banks to continue their functions to take care of the distribution of food and household necessities and the payment of payrolls.

This bank holiday, while resulting in many cases in great inconvenience, is affording us the opportunity to supply the currency necessary to meet the situation. **No sound bank is a dollar worse off than it was when it closed its doors last Monday. Neither is any bank which may turn out not to be in a position for immediate opening.** The new law allows the twelve Federal Reserve Banks to issue additional currency on good assets and thus the banks which reopen will be able to meet every legitimate call. **The new currency is being sent out by the Bureau of Engraving and Printing in large volume to every part of the country. It is sound currency because it is backed by actual, good assets.**

A question you will ask is this: why are all the banks not to be reopened at the same time? The answer is simple. Your government does not intend that the history of the past few years shall be repeated. We do not want and will not have another epidemic of bank failures.

As a result, we start tomorrow, Monday, with the opening of banks in the twelve Federal Reserve Bank cities — those banks which on first examination by the treasury have already been found to be all right. This will be followed on Tuesday by the resumption of all their functions by banks already found to be sound in cities where there are recognized clearing houses. That means about 250 cities of the United states.

On Wednesday and succeeding days banks in smaller places all through the country will resume business, subject, of course, to the government's physical ability to complete its survey. It is necessary that the reopening of banks be extended over a period in order to permit the banks to make applications for necessary loans, to obtain currency needed to meet their requirements and to enable the government to make common sense checkups.

Let me make it clear to you that if your bank does not open the first day you are by no means justified in believing that it will not open. A bank that opens on one of the subsequent days is in exactly the same status as the bank that opens tomorrow.

I know that many people are worrying about state banks not members of the Federal Reserve System. These banks can and will receive assistance from members banks and from the Reconstruction Finance Corporation. These state banks are following the same course as the national banks except that they get their licenses to resume business from the state authorities, and these authorities have been asked by the Secretary of the Treasury to permit their good banks to open up on the same schedule as the national banks. I am confident that the state banking departments will be as careful as the national government in the policy relating to the opening of banks and will follow the same broad policy.

It is possible that when the banks resume a very few people who have not recovered from their fear may again begin withdrawals. Let me make it clear that the banks will take care of all needs — and it is my belief that hoarding during the past week has become an exceedingly unfashionable pastime. It needs no prophet to tell you that when the people find that they can get their money — that they can get it when they want it for all legitimate purposes — the phantom of fear will soon be laid. **People will again be glad to have their money where it will be safely taken care of and where they can use it conveniently at any time. I can assure you that it is safer to keep your money in a reopened bank than under the mattress.**

The success of our whole great national program depends, of course, upon the cooperation of the public — on its intelligent support and use of a reliable system.

Remember that the essential accomplishment of the new legislation is that it makes it possible for banks more readily to convert their assets into cash than was the case before. More liberal provision has been made for banks to borrow on these assets at the Reserve Banks and more liberal provision has also been made for issuing currency on the security of those good assets. **This currency is not fiat currency. It is issued only on adequate security—and every good bank has an abundance of such security.**

One more point before I close. There will be, of course, some banks unable to reopen without being reorganized. The new law allows the government to assist in making these reorganizations quickly and effectively and even allows the government to subscribe to at least a part of new capital which may be required.

I hope you can see from this elemental recital of what your government is doing that there is nothing complex, or radical, in the process.

We had a bad banking situation. Some of our bankers had shown themselves either incompetent or dishonest in their handling of the people's funds. They had used the money entrusted to them in speculations and unwise loans. This was, of course, not true in the vast majority of our banks, but it was true in enough of them to shock the people for a time into a sense of insecurity and to put them into a frame of mind where they did not differentiate, but seemed to assume that the acts of a comparative few had tainted them all. It was the government's job to straighten out this situation and do it as quickly as possible—and the job is being performed.

I do not promise you that every bank will be reopened or that individual losses will not be suffered, but there will be no losses that possibly could be avoided; and there would have been more and greater losses had we continued to drift. I can even promise you salvation for some at least of the sorely pressed banks. We shall be engaged not merely in reopening sound banks but in the creation of sound banks through reorganization.

It has been wonderful to me to catch the note of confidence from all over the country. I can never be sufficiently grateful to the people for the loyal support they have given me in their acceptance of the judgment that has dictated our course, even though all our processes may not have seemed clear to them.

After all, there is an element in the readjustment of our financial system more important than currency, more important than gold, and that is the confidence of the people. Confidence and courage are the essentials of success in carrying out our plan. You people must have faith; you must not be stampeded by rumors or guesses. Let us unite in banishing fear. We have provided the machinery to restore our financial system; it is up to you to support and make it work.

It is your problem no less than it is mine. Together we cannot fail.

LESSON 2:
RISK AND REWARD
IN CAN'T STOP

O ne of the key elements of a financial plan is an investment strategy to help grow wealth over time. Individual investors must carefully consider the level of risk they are comfortable with in relation to potential returns. Retirement savings accounts, for example, make use of low-risk investments that bring in modest returns over a very long period of time. Other investors are able and willing to consider higher-risk investments for a chance to gain larger returns. Sid Sackson's classic game Can't Stop explores risk management, return on investment, and your level of comfort with risk.

FINANCIAL LITERACY INFORMATION

ASSESSING RISK

In Can't Stop, players are attempting to move pawns across a game board within columns numbered from 2 to 12 for each of the possible sums that can result from rolling two standard six-sided dice—an action gamers refer to as rolling 2d6. Each turn, players roll 4d6 and then combine the die results into two pairs of summed dice. For example, a roll resulting in dice showing 1, 3, 4, and 5 could be combined in pairs to produce the sums of 4 and 9 (formed by 1+3 and 4+5), 5 and 8 (1+4 and 3+5), or 6 and 7 (1+5 and 3+4). Players pick a pair of sums and move the temporary pawns forward on those columns...and then the real math of the game happens. Roll again? Or stop?

There is a great deal of math at work in this deceptively simple game. The board is a hexagon, not just to look like a stop sign, but to accommodate the short and long columns that portray the probabilities of the results from rolling 2d6. There are 36 possible combinations of dice rolls with distribution forming a bell curve ranging from 2 to 12 with like percentages for each pair ranging up and down from the center result of 7. The probabilities are depicted on the game board by the length of the columns and number of moves needed to reach the top and capture the column. For example, it takes only three moves to capture the 2 or 12 columns, but the chance of those numbers being rolled is quite low, only 13 percent In comparison, the longest column under number 7 has 12 spaces, but rolling 2d6 has a 64 percent chance to result in a 7. Understanding the math behind the game board can help players make a more informed decision about risk assessment. There have actually been master's theses written on Can't Stop that go into further detail on when to roll and when to stop. The game is often used as an example of risk assessment.

In financial terms, risk assessment uses complicated math to measure risk based on the expected level of loss and the potential for a given threat happening. On the two extremes one could face a risk that would result in a high level of loss that has a low chance of happening, or a risk with a low level of loss that has a high chance of happening. Encourage students to think about two tools that they might use on a daily basis. We put special, often very expensive, cases on our phones to protect them in the case of a drop. Though there is a low chance of that happening, there is a high level of loss if the phone's screen cracks. On the other hand, we treat most pens and pencils with a very casual attitude. There is a high chance that they will break, but the level of loss is negligible in most cases.

This type of risk assessment drives the insurance industry. Insurers use actuarial science to carefully consider risks in terms of level of loss and potential of happening. Anyone who lives near a lake or river understands this quite well. Their level of risk for catastrophic loss from flooding is so high that insurance companies often will not insure them. Homeowners have to use a special flood insurance offering from the federal government that is quite costly. On the other hand, mobile phone companies offer insurance for phones breaking for a very low monthly cost. They have determined that, given the number of people buying insurance (and the number of people to whom they also sell expensive protective cases) there is an acceptable level of risk in this business. This is a critical determination as all businesses and financial transactions carry some level of risk. The hard part is determining whether the level of risk is acceptable or not.

RETURN ON INVESTMENT

A second key concept in determining acceptable levels of risk is the potential for return on investment, or ROI. ROI is a measurement typically expressed as a percentage of gains made as profit compared to an initial investment. It is calculated by dividing the net profit by the initial investment and then multiplying the result by 100 to express it as a percentage. For example, if someone invests $100 and receives a $10 profit, they had a 10 percent ROI. This can be a dangerous and deceptive calculation, though. Every time someone buys a $1 lottery ticket thinking about the potential for millions of dollars in return on their $1 investment they may have correctly considered the math of ROI but are ignoring the bigger picture. Though there is a chance of a very large return on a small investment, there is an incredibly small chance of that return actually paying out. In the New York Lottery Mega Millions game, the chance of correctly guessing all five numbers as well as the mega ball number is 1 in 258,890,850 or about 1 in 260 million.[1] The problem is that whenever we think about the lottery we think about that one smiling person on the news holding up the big check. We don't think of the hundreds of millions of losing tickets that were torn up and thrown away in disgust. Physicist Richard Feynman discussed this problem once in a lecture:

> "You know, the most amazing thing happened to me tonight. I was coming here, on the way to the lecture, and I came in through the parking lot. And you won't believe what happened. I saw a car with the license plate ARW 357. Can you imagine? Of all the millions of license plates in the state, what was the chance I would see that particular one tonight? Amazing!"[2]

What Feynman meant is that of course it wasn't really amazing that he saw a particular license plate; it was just that he called attention to something that happened. Players will justify their low risk of $1 a day by dreaming of a huge possible payout but fail to think about the fact that they are actually losing a great deal of money. The chance of winning back the $1 investment is only 1 in 21; $2 win odds are 1 in 56. Therefore, over a single year of playing every day, players can reasonably expect to end up winning somewhere around $25. An ROI of negative $340 or -93 percent.

To really think about ROI, we have to also consider the viability of the investment. Playing the lottery offers an incredible potential return, but with a very low chance of paying out. To be a truly effective measurement, ROI needs to consider both risk and reward.

RISK VS. REWARD

A modern savings account at a bank secured by the United States Federal Deposit Insurance Corporation (FDIC) is an exemplar of a low-risk, low-reward investment. Through the FDIC, the government insures an individual's deposits up to $250,000 against the risk of bank failure. The mitigation of risk also means a drastic reduction in rewards. Most savings accounts today offer only around one percent annual return. There are many other investment possibilities available. Certificates of deposit (CDs) require that individuals deposit their money for a specific length of time. The FDIC also insures these accounts; risk actually comes from the individual betting that he or she won't need access to the money for the length of the CD. Early withdrawal involves severe penalties in most cases. In return for this extra risk, though, individuals can expect a higher interest level and thus greater returns. Larger deposits and longer CD terms typically offer greater rewards.

The two above examples involve very minimal risk. The federal government insures the deposits, so there isn't any real risk of loss. If you want greater rewards, though, you have to accept greater risk. Investing in the stock market is a common way of growing assets over time. Pension plans and retirement plans use carefully calculated risks within the stock market to grow wealth over time. Unlike an individual stock trader, these massive plans have enormous pools of money allowing them to better control their exposure to risk. Behind the scenes, fund managers spread money across low-, medium-, and high-risk investments. By using some high-risk investments buffered by lower risk options, the managers can hope for some larger returns on investment without betting everything on a single roll of the dice. This is the real science of risk assessment and return on investment— a careful management of low- and high-risk actions that combine together to provide a steady, predictable return over time. This isn't about luck or passion, this is about math.

LESSON PLAN 2A

ESSENTIAL QUESTION

What is the relationship between risk and reward?

VOCABULARY

The following vocabulary words are important concepts for the content in this lesson:
- Risk
- Reward
- Return on investment
- Actuarial

SUGGESTED READING RESOURCES

Other Sources:
Smart Strategies for Investing Wisely and Successfully
Written by Judy Monroe Peterson
Published by Rosen Publishing Group, Inc., 2014
ISBN: 9781477776186

MINI READING LESSON

While you are reading the available text material or the suggested reading resources, attempt to answer the following question: Why is it important to consider the potentials for risk and rewards when considering financial decisions? Introduce the vocabulary words on the previous page. They can be introduced even if they are not in the specific reading you have chosen.

GUIDED PRACTICE

Have students preview any headings and subheadings in the reading they have been asked to do. Have students read the selections.

Read and Discuss

Have students reread each section of the text and discuss the following:
- How do you determine risk in your daily life?
- Why is it critical to think about chance of actually obtaining a reward, not just looking at the possible return for an investment?
- In looking at the fine print from an advertisement on an investing opportunity, how are risk and reward addressed?

MODEL

Have the students play the game following the rules as written. This should ideally be done prior to any discussion about risk, reward, and return on investment. The goal is to have students approach the game as naïve investors who let their passions dictate actions. After this first play-through, ask students to journal their thoughts and motivations during game play. Did they have a strategy? How did they decide whether to stop or roll?

INDEPENDENT PRACTICE

After the readings and discussion, have students play the game again. What new strategies and understandings did they have for the second game? Have them record a second journal entry about the new experience.

Writing Activities

Narrative: Write a dialog between two friends standing in the checkout line at a gas station. The first person is planning on buying a daily lottery ticket. The second person is not.

Express an Opinion: Should you buy a protective case for your phone? Should you buy the offered insurance from the phone company? Support your answer.

SHARING/REFLECTION

Have individuals or groups share and discuss their work with the class.

ASSESSMENT

Collect completed formative assessment (activity for model section) and writing activities and review. The second journal entry should reflect a deeper understanding of the game as an example of risk and reward. The narrative will be basic for now but will be revisited and updated in the second lesson to include math. The opinion piece should include some thoughts on the student's personal feelings about risk.

EXTENSION ACTIVITIES

Further Research: Have students look up the interest rates and returns on investment for different savings, CDs, and other financial options at a local bank.

Further Research: Explore an aspect of risk analysis or actuarial science for an insurance company to see how risk professionals approach what seems like random events.

LESSON PLAN 2B

Essential Question

What is the math behind risk assessment?

Vocabulary

The following vocabulary words are important concepts for the content in this lesson:

- Risk assessment
- Probability
- Actuary tables
- Probability tables
- Risk aversion

Suggested Reading Resources

Other Sources:
Smart Strategies for Investing Wisely and Successfully
Written by Judy Monroe Peterson
Published by Rosen Publishing Group, Inc., 2014
ISBN:9781477776186

Mini Reading Lesson

While you are reading the available text material or the suggested reading resources, attempt to answer the following question: How does math affect playing games like Can't Stop? Introduce the vocabulary words above. They can be introduced even if they are not in the specific reading you have chosen.

GUIDED PRACTICE

Have students preview any headings and subheadings in the reading they have been asked to do. Have students read the selections.

Read and Discuss

Have students reread each section of the text and discuss the following:

- How are probability tables generated?
- How can we use probability tables to inform our decisions?
- Why might some people be more prone toward risk aversion than others?
- Thinking personally, how comfortable are you with pressing your luck on rolling the dice if the probability table suggests that you should continue rolling?

MODEL

Reintroduce the board for Can't Stop and explain how it models the probability table of results for rolling 2d6. Share the probability table for the game available online at www.teachingthroughgames.com. The table includes a column suggesting the number of times that one could safely continue rolling for each combination of three working columns within a turn of the game. Map students risk aversion on a linear continuum by asking students to rate their aversion ranging from 1 (go for it!) to 10 (not so sure about this). To explore risk aversion, select three different combinations of numbers from the probability table—ideally, ones that offer low, medium, and high risk—and then have three students roll 2d6 for the suggested number of times as shown in the table as an example for the group. Based on these results, have students think about how they felt during the exercise. How comfortable are they with the risk? As the rolls progress, students can move their marker up or down the range on the continuum. At the end of the exercise, have them write a short reflection on why their risk aversion changed or did not change through the rolls.

INDEPENDENT PRACTICE

Have students play the game again, but this time make the probability tables for rolling 2d6 available for reference. How does this change their strategy for success in Can't Stop? Journal after this play experience as well. Ask them to consider if the game is still fun if they are just following the probability table? Or was it more fun when they were just flying by the seat of their pants? After using the table to play the game, have the students play the game a final time without the table, but with the knowledge of probability and potential return on investment for each of the rolls. Complete the journal by reflecting on this final play experience and how it might inform their financial decisions in life.

Writing Activities

Remind students of the vocabulary introduced for their reading and ask them to attempt to include that vocabulary in appropriate ways in the writing activities they do.

> **Narrative:** Update the dialog from the first lesson, but this time add in math to support the arguments being made by the two people involved.
>
> **Inform or Explain:** Explain how probability works. Select a row from the three number chart in the Can't Stop probability table and test it twenty times to see if the suggestion for number of rolls is accurate. Record all rolls in a table and then calculate the rate of success. Reflect on this and explain how it might support or disprove actuarial science.
>
> **Express an Opinion:** Should governments support lotteries?

SHARING/REFLECTION

Have individuals or groups share and discuss their work with the class.

Assessment

Collect completed formative assessment (activity for model section) and writing activities and review. The journal entries should show clear evidence of growth over the two lessons including a much deeper understanding of probability and risk. The updates to the dialog should include math as supporting evidence and therefore should likely conclude that playing the lottery as anything but a game for fun is not a good investment of money. For the explanation, a sophisticated answer will conclude that twenty tests is much too small of a sample and that actuarial science works because it considers enormous groups. The opinion will result in different answers.

Extension Activities

Further Research: Which is more likely? Dying in an airplane accident or as you drive to the airport? Why are we afraid of things that are very unlikely to happen? How do these fears drive legislation?

LESSON 3:
STOCK MARKETS IN PANIC ON WALL STREET!

Players will need to bring all of their new risk assessment and return on investment measurement skills to bear as they navigate the stock market in Panic on Wall Street! (Grouper Games, 2011). This game simulates an open outcry stock market similar to the New York Stock Exchange; buyers and sellers of stock will be negotiating prices simultaneously in a chaotic frenzy of stock trading.

FINANCIAL LITERACY INFORMATION

HISTORY OF STOCKS

The concept of buying and selling shares of stock—documents representing a portion of the equity, or worth, of a company—is not new. In fact, it is quite medieval. Mining companies in France and Sweden sold shares of their mining operations in the thirteenth century. The first example of a modern, publicly traded company was the Dutch East India Company, founded in 1602 as a joint-stock company publicly traded on the Amsterdam Stock Exchange. Joint-stock companies sell shares of stock that are then purchased by shareholders. The number of shares held by different shareholders determines the percentage of their ownership in the company. For early trading companies that faced grave danger on each voyage to sea, having a larger group of shareholders across whom the risk could be spread was a great benefit. No longer was a single merchant rolling the dice on every voyage; instead the larger company could mitigate losses by selling shares in the potential profit. These payouts to shareholders, called dividends, made successful voyages less profitable for the company itself but also ensured long-term survival even if cargos were lost.

Instead of a small business with a single owner and operator, joint-stock companies are owned and governed by the shareholders. They elect a board of directors to oversee the company and ensure that the value of the shares of stock will continue to grow. But what if the value of the stock declines? In 1609, a Dutch merchant named Issac Le Maire figured out a new way to make money even as stock prices fell. He invented the short sale; the practice of selling a stock, waiting for it to decline in price, and then repurchasing the stock at the newly lowered price. This has been a controversial aspect of stock trading since its inception. Another way that investors can protect themselves is to purchase bonds instead of stocks. Stocks give the shareholder a percentage of ownership in the company whereas bonds are just loans. Bondholders will receive the same amount of re-payment regardless of whether or not the company is successful. In the case of an extreme failure forcing a company to close, bonds have to be repaid before stocks. Bonds are a much lower risk type of investment that offers a higher level of safety with a lower chance of return. Stocks have a chance for much higher returns but at much higher risk. If the company does well and the stock value continues to rise the stockholder makes money. The stock market is a risk, though. It doesn't always go up.

GLITCHES IN THE STOCK MARKET

Sometimes stock markets can develop a glitch. Sometimes, as we will shortly see, prices suddenly crash. Other times, though, stock prices continue to rise far beyond what could even be imagined as reasonable. This is called a bubble market; a name that should serve as a warning regarding the very fragile nature of the growth. The market seems to keep expanding and expanding until suddenly it pops. One of the most famous bubble markets in history happened in the Netherlands from November 1636 until the spring of 1637. In a time known as Tulipmania, the price of tulip bulbs rose rapidly amidst rampant speculation only to fall sharply a few months later. A more recent bubble market can be seen in the dot-com boom and bust of the late 1990s. From 1997 to 1999 hundreds of new Internet companies were founded and listed for sale on the NASDAQ, a technology trading market in the United States.

Many of the start-ups failed, but Pets.com was one of the most spectacular burnouts. Pets.com was first listed with the NASDAQ in an initial public offering (IPO) in February of 2000 and was out of business before the end of the year. In this case, it wasn't a failure of the stock market, but a specific failure within the way Pets.com did business. The bubble market mentality with investors looking to buy shares in anything technology related meant that the really bad business ideas developed by Pets.com were allowed to continue. Outside of a bubble market, the business would never have had a chance to grow. When the dot-com bubble burst Pets.com simply couldn't survive. Other companies lost a great deal of stock value when the technology bubble popped but managed to survive and thrive in the following years. For example, shares for Amazon.com fell from a peak of $107 per share during the bubble to only $7 a share.

Even without a specific bubble market, a sudden panic among investors can trigger a massive selloff and send stock prices tumbling. In late October 1929, after years of profits and steady growth, the New York Stock Exchange crashed. The market, the collection of stocks bought and sold at the exchange, lost over $30 billon on October 28 and 29. As newspapers spread word of the collapse, many articles stressed the inherent risks in stock markets. On October 30, the *New York Times* published a review of articles from around the country:

Hartford Courant—"The panicky tsate [sic] of mind is purely psychological. Out of the depths are heard calls for help by the Federal Reserve Board. This is not a function of the Federal Reserve."

Louisville Courier-Journal—"Such a commotion has been long overdue as the logical result of excessive speculation which has pushed up and kept up prices to figures which in many instances were artificial."

St. Louis Post-Dispatch—"Since the stock market never did represent anything better than chance, it is not reasonable to suppose that the mischance of a day is going to make it very much different. There is always plenty of chance."[3]

As it turned out, the mischance of those few days in October 1929 led the United States into the Great Depression, a time of financial ruin that lasted for most of the following decade.

PLAYING THE MARKET

In Panic on Wall Street, players take on the role of either a company manager offering stock or a speculator buying stock. Rather than an exact simulation of a stock market, it is a lighter game meant to provide an engaging experience that highlights the chaos and confusion of speculation gone wild. Within the game, there are four colors of stock available: blue has the lowest risk followed by green, yellow, and then the very high-risk red stocks. After stocks are sold each round, dice will be rolled to determine the movement of stock prices in the market. As the lowest risk stock, the price for blue can either move up or down a single space or stay the same. With a value ranging from only $20 to $40 across the board, there is low risk but also very low reward. Red stocks, on the other hand, are incredibly high risk but offer the potential for huge rewards. On any roll of the die, the value of red stocks can move seven spaces. That means the stock can go from the high of $70 to the lowest value at -$20 in a single turn. Suddenly speculators hoping for a big payout with a $70 stock could end up owing the bank $20 for each share they bought. This is an example of a failed short sale. In the lessons we will look at other ways in which Panic on Wall Street can help students understand how stock markets work and how to invest wisely.

LESSON PLAN 3A

ESSENTIAL QUESTION

How does the stock market work?

VOCABULARY

The following vocabulary words are important concepts for the content in this lesson:
- Stock
- Share
- Bond

- Equity
- Stock market
- Short sale
- Valuation

SUGGESTED READING RESOURCES

Primary Source Document:
"A Brief History of the 1987 Stock Market Crash," by Mark Carlson. This document is included after the lesson in an annotated form with vocabulary underlined and some important passages for close reading highlighted; it is available online at www.teachingthroughgames.com for printing.

Other Sources:
How the Stock Market Works (Real World Economics).
Written by Kathy Furgang
Published by Rosen Publishing Group, Inc., 2010
ISBN: 9781435894662

MINI READING LESSON

While you are reading the available text material or the suggested reading resources, attempt to answer the following question: Why did companies start selling equity shares on stock markets? Introduce the vocabulary words above. They can be introduced even if they are not in the specific reading you have chosen.

GUIDED PRACTICE

Have students preview any headings and subheadings in the reading they have been asked to do. Have students read the selections. After reading about stock markets, introduce Panic on Wall Street. For this first lesson, players will be stepping through the game in a controlled fashion. The regular rules of the game are designed to encourage the much more chaotic reality of an open outcry trading floor.

First, introduce the game pieces. Talk about the stock market as depicted on the price board. Review the different levels of risk and reward associated with each color of stock. A key concept for investing in stocks is valuation. Experts have to decide how much a company is worth and therefore how much each individual share of stock is worth. Valuation depends on a company's assets and debts as well as predications of future performance. In the game, players have to carefully consider the value of different stocks. While the red stock may be worth $50 during the stock selling phase, the dice will be rolled and the actual value will change before payout. The red die has faces that will either raise or lower the stock price two, three, or even seven spaces. Players have to carefully consider how much they want to risk in buying the stock. Is it really worth $50? Or does the risk associated drive the cost lower?

As a group exercise, have students perform a valuation on a single share of each color of stock. Use the starting prices on the game board; $30 for each color. Have students work in a small group to discuss and determine an optimal bid price for each stock. How much do they want to pay for a share of each color of stock? Then, roll the dice and see what happens.

Read and Discuss

Have students reread each section of the text and discuss the following:

- What aspects of each color of stock influenced your valuation?
- Did everyone in your group have a similar level of comfort with risk?
- How did the depiction of the stock market in Panic on Wall Street match with what you read and learned about stock markets?
- How is the rolling of the dice similar to or different from what happens in the stock market?

MODEL

Now, have students play Panic on Wall Street using a modified rule set.

For this first full game, instead of the chaos of an open outcry trading floor, use a more structured bidding method. Within the investor group and the manager group, determine two start players. The manager start player will advance one of his or her stocks for consideration. Then, starting with the investor start player, that player can either bid or pass. Bidding continues in a clockwise rotation around the investors until only one bidder remains and everyone else has passed. Even if an investor passes, he or she can come back into the bidding for the same stock but might lose out if only one other player bids. Repeat with the next manager in order advancing a share for consideration. The new start player for the investors is the person who bought the last stock. This will greatly lengthen the turns in the game, and so you might only be able to complete one or two turns. Still, it provides a very solid foundation for when the game moves into full chaos mode. Have investors and managers record their transactions on a balance sheet so they can track the rise (and fall?) of their fortunes.

INDEPENDENT PRACTICE

Remind students of the vocabulary introduced for their reading and ask them to attempt to include that vocabulary in appropriate ways in the writing activities they do.

Writing Activities

Narrative: You are a Dutch merchant trader in the sixteenth century. Write a conversation that might have taken place as you explain the concept of equity shares in your trading company to a potential investor. What concerns might the investor have? How will you introduce this new concept?

Inform or Explain: In Panic on Wall Street, the dice introduce a huge element of chance for stock prices. Research what role chance plays in the real stock market. Explain a situation in which chance, not the actions of the company, caused a massive change in a stock price.

Express an Opinion: What is the best approach to investing, low-risk stocks or high-risk stocks? Explain and defend your answer.

SHARING/REFLECTION

Have individuals or groups share and discuss their work with the class.

ASSESSMENT

Collect completed formative assessment (activity for model section) and writing activities and review. For the game play, review the balance sheets for the investors and managers. They should correctly display transactions and show a starting and ending balance. For the narrative piece, students should include a discussion of the risks and rewards of investing. Important points to be raised include the idea of spreading out risk across more investors while also sharing rewards, the idea that equity shares grant part ownership, and a clear warning about risk. For the opinion, answers will vary. A sophisticated answer will recommend a balanced approach that includes some high-risk and some low-risk investments as a way to protect wealth while still having a chance for faster growth.

EXTENSION ACTIVITIES

Further Research: What else is traded besides equity stocks? Have students explore commodity markets, futures trading, and bond markets.

Important Details: Have students identify ten important details to know about how stock markets work and justify their choices of those details using the Important Details sheet in the appendix and available online at www.teachingthroughgames.com for printing. Answers will vary.

A BRIEF HISTORY OF THE 1987 STOCK MARKET CRASH

A Brief History of the 1987 Stock Market Crash with a Discussion of the Federal Reserve Response
Mark Carlson, 2006. Published by the Federal Reserve and available in the public domain.

On October 19, 1987, the stock market, along with the associated futures and options markets, crashed, with the S&P 500 stock market index falling about 20 percent. The market crash of 1987 is a significant event not just because of the swiftness and severity of the market decline, but also because it showed the weaknesses of the trading systems themselves and how they could be strained and come close to breaking in extreme conditions. The problems in the trading systems interacted with the price declines to make the crisis worse. One notable problem was the difficulty gathering information in the rapidly changing and chaotic environment. The systems in place simply were not capable of processing so many transactions at once.[1] Uncertainty about information likely contributed to a pull back by investors from the market. Another factor was the record margin calls that accompanied the large price changes. While necessary to protect the solvency of the clearinghouse processing the trades, the size of the margin calls and the timing of payments served to reduce market liquidity. Finally, some have argued that "program trades," which led to notable volumes of large securities sales contributed to overwhelming the system.

The Federal Reserve was active in providing highly visible liquidity support in an effort to bolster market functioning. In particular, the Federal Reserve eased short-term credit conditions by conducting more expansive open market operations at earlier-than-usual times, issuing public statements affirming its commitment to providing liquidity, and temporarily liberalizing the rules governing the lending of Treasury securities from its portfolio. The liquidity support was important by itself, but the public nature of the activities likely helped support market confidence. The Federal Reserve also encouraged the commercial banking system to extend liquidity support to other financial market participants.[2] The response of the Federal Reserve was well received and was seen as important in helping financial markets return to more normal functioning.

The purpose of this paper is to provide a useful history of the 1987 stock market crash and the factors contributing to its severity and also to illustrate some of the tools the Federal Reserve has at its disposal to deal with financial crises. Section 1 of the paper provides some pertinent

---

[1] These systems have all been upgraded dramatically since the 1987 crash. Indeed, the crash may have provided some impetus for the upgrades.

[2] These activities are discussed in Greenspan (1988).

2

background information on developments in equity markets and trading strategies preceding the crash. A timeline of the crisis is presented in Section 2. Section 3 discusses some factors that contributed to the severity of the crisis and that threatened market functioning. Section 4 details the actions taken by the Federal Reserve. Section 5 concludes.

1   Background

During the years prior to the crash, equity markets had been posting strong gains (see Figure 1). Price increases outpaced earnings growth and lifted price-earnings ratios; some commentators warned that the market had become overvalued (see for example Wall Street Journal (1987a) and Anders and Garcia (1987)). There had been an influx of new investors, such as pension funds, into the stock market during the 1980s, and the increased demand helped support prices (Katzenbach 1987). Equities were also boosted by some favorable tax treatments given to the financing of corporate buyouts, such as allowing firms to deduct interest expenses associated with debt issued during a buyout, which increased the number of companies that were potential takeover targets and pushed up their stock prices (Presidential Task Force on Market Mechanisms (Brady Report) 1988).

Figure 1:

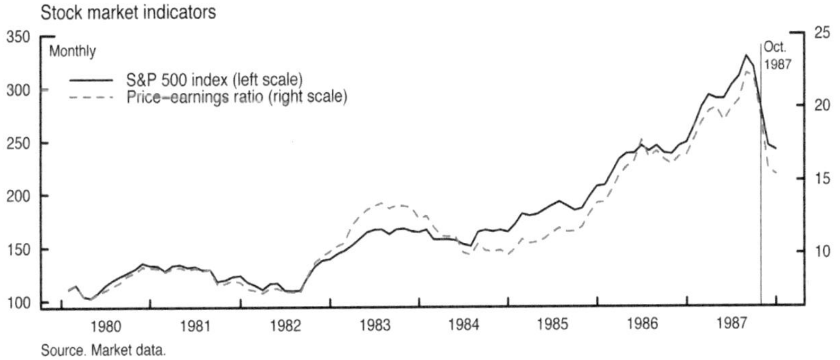

Stock market indicators

Source. Market data.

3

45

However, the macroeconomic outlook during the months leading up to the crash had become somewhat less certain. Interest rates were rising globally. A growing U.S. trade deficit and decline in the value of the dollar were leading to concerns about inflation and the need for higher interest rates in the U.S. as well (Winkler and Herman 1987).

Importantly, financial markets had seen an increase in the use of "program trading" strategies, where computers were set up to quickly trade particular amounts of a large number of stocks, such as those in a particular stock index, when certain conditions were met.[3] There were two program trading strategies that have often been tied to the stock market crash. The first was "portfolio insurance," which was supposed to limit the losses investors might face from a declining market. Under this strategy, computer models were used to compute optimal stock-to-cash ratios at various market prices. Broadly, the models would suggest that the investor decrease the weight on stocks during falling markets, thereby reducing exposure to the falling market, while during rising markets the models would suggest an increased weight on stocks. Buying portfolio insurance was similar to buying a put option in that it allowed investors to preserve upside gains but limit downside risk. In practice, many portfolio insurers conducted their operations in the futures market rather than in the cash market. By buying stock index futures in a rising market and selling them in a falling market, portfolio insurers could provide protection against losses from falling equity prices without trading stocks. Trading in the futures market was generally preferred as it was cheaper and many of the institutions that provided portfolio insurance were not authorized to trade their clients' stock (Brady Report 1988, p. 7). Portfolio insurers did not continually update their analysis about the optimal portfolio of stocks and cash holdings, as the procedure was time consuming and transaction costs could add up with constant re-optimizing; instead, portfolio insurers ran the models periodically and then traded in batches (Garcia 1987). There were concerns that the use of portfolio insurance could lead many investors to sell stocks and futures simultaneously; there was an article in the Wall Street Journal on October 12 citing concerns that during a declining stock market, the use of portfolio insurance "could snowball into a stunning rout for stocks" (Garcia 1987).

---

[3]See also Katzenbach (1987), who provides a detailed description of the different types of program trading strategies described here.

4

The second program trading strategy was "index arbitrage," which was designed to produce profits by exploiting discrepancies between the value of stocks in an index and the value of the stock-index futures contracts. If the value of the stocks was lower than the value of the futures contract, then index arbitragers would buy the stocks in the cash market and sell the futures contract knowing that the prices would have to converge at the time the futures contract expired. The reverse transactions could be executed if the value of stocks was above that of the futures contract; however, rules restricting short-sales made this trade more difficult to implement for arbitragers that did not own stocks (Katzenbach 1987, p. 12).[4]

The use of program trading was facilitated on the New York Stock Exchange (NYSE) by the use of the designated order turnaround (DOT) system (Katzenbach 1987). This order processing system allowed NYSE member firms to transmit large volumes of buy and sell orders through their own connections to the NYSE common message switch and have them routed to a specialist/trading post.[5] If the specialist did not report execution of the trade within three minutes, the NYSE gave confirmation of execution at a reference price. If the trade was not made with a third party, then the trade was put on the specialist's account (Brady Report 1988, Study VI, p. 11). The automatic nature of the DOT system enabled it to handle the large number of trades needed for the successful implementation of program trading strategies.

2   Timeline of the crash

The review of the crash presented here focuses on developments at the NYSE and on the the Chicago Mercantile Exchange (CME) and the Chicago Board of Trade (CBOT), exchanges where options and futures for popular stock indexes, such as the S&P 500, were traded.[6]

---

[4]The Securities Exchange Act Rule 10a-1 prohibited short sales of the stocks when the bid price was lower than the last reported trading price.

[5]A specialist at the NYSE is an exchange member in charge of making a market in a particular stock or stocks. All stocks are assigned to a specialist. The specialist has a monopoly on arranging the market for the stocks and in return has an obligation to make a market when there are order imbalances by buying/selling when there are numerous sell/buy orders from other market participants (Saunders and Cornett 2007, p. 259).

[6]There were also notable problems in the over-the-counter stock market. Market makers in the over-the-counter market were not obligated to maintain an orderly market and many withdrew from trading. Delays in processing trades resulted in investors receiving prices very different from what they expected. Many brokers did not answer

5

2.1 Wednesday, October 14 - Friday, October 16, 1987

Two events Wednesday morning have been pointed to as precipitating a decline in the stock market that continued for the rest of the week. First, news organizations reported that the Ways and Means Committee of the U.S. House of Representatives had filed legislation to eliminate tax benefits associated with financing mergers (Securities and Exchange Commission (SEC) Report 1988, p. 3-10).[7] Stocks' values were reassessed as investors reduced the odds that certain companies would be take-over targets. Second, the Commerce Department's announcement of the trade deficit for August was notably above expectations. On this news, the dollar declined and expectations that the Federal Reserve would tighten policy increased (Wall Street Journal 1987b). Interest rates rose, putting further downward pressure on equity prices (see Figure 2).

Figure 2:

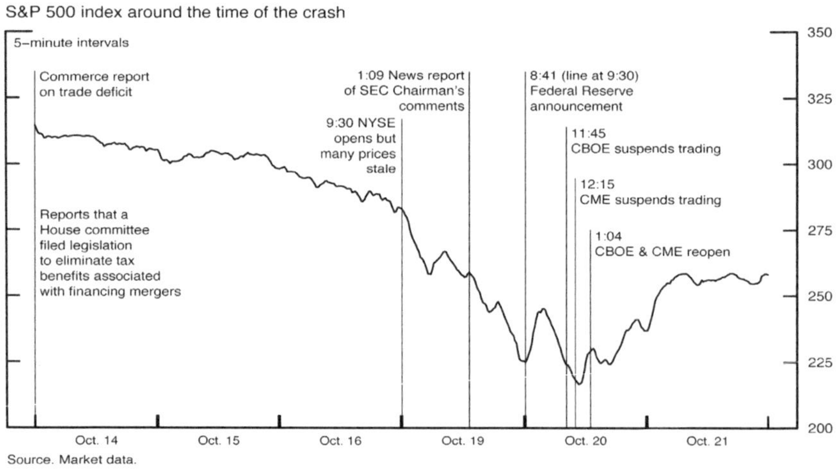

S&P 500 index around the time of the crash

Source. Market data.

their phones, leaving investors unable to reach them. Erratic price movements and quotes resulted in frequent lock-ups in the electronic trading system used in the over-the-counter market. For further details on the problems in the over-the-counter market see the discussion in the Brady Report (1998, Study VI, pp. 49-63).

[7]The proposal would have eliminated the tax deductions for some interest expenses and would have started taxing "greenmail"—payments made by companies to corporate raiders to buy back their stock at above-market prices to prevent the raider from taking over the company.

6

On Thursday, equity markets continued to decline. Some of this decrease was attributed to anxiety among institutions, especially pension funds, and among individual investors, which led to a movement of funds from stocks into the relative safety of bonds (Wall Street Journal 1987c). There was also heavy selling during the last half hour of the day amid heavier-than-usual activity by portfolio insurers (Brady Report 1988, p. 21).

Markets continued to decline on Friday, as ongoing anxiety was augmented by some technical factors. A variety of stock index options expired on Friday; price movements during the previous two days had eliminated many at-the-money options so that investors could not easily roll their positions into new contracts for hedging purposes. These developments pushed more investors into the futures markets, where they sold futures contracts as a hedge against falling stocks.[8] Increased sales of futures contracts created a price discrepancy between the value of the stock index in the futures market and the value of the stocks on the NYSE. Index arbitrage traders reportedly took advantage of this price discrepancy to buy futures and sell stocks, which transmitted the downward pressures to the NYSE (Brady Report 1988, Study III, p. 12).

By the end of the day on Friday, markets had fallen considerably, with the S&P 500 down over nine percent for the week. This decrease was one of the largest one-week declines of the preceeding couple of decades, and it helped set the stage for the turmoil the following week (Wall Street Journal 1987d). Portfolio insurers were left with an "overhang" as their models suggested that they should sell more stocks or futures contracts (SEC Report 1988, p. 2-10). Mutual funds experienced redemptions and needed to sell shares (Brady Report 1988, p. 29).[9] Further, some aggressive institutions anticipated the portfolio insurance sales and mutual fund redemptions and wanted to pre-empt the sales by selling first (Brady Report 1988, p. 29; SEC Report 1988, p. 3-12).[10] There were some signs that futures markets were already starting to feel the effects of

---

[8]This activity was similar to the technique used by portfolio insurers.

[9]The SEC (1988, pp. 2-17—2-18) indicated that these sales were largely attributable to one major mutual fund complex.

[10]While there were some concerns about institutions frontrunning customer accounts during the crash (see SEC Report 1988, pp. 3-30—3-33), that need not be the case described here. Institutions with knowledge of how portfolio insurance models worked, or that read newspapers with stories of investor concern about the market decline (for instance the Wall Street Journal (1987c, Oct. 16)), may well have guessed that other institutions would be entering

7

heavier-than-usual volumes, with traders on the Chicago Mercantile Exchange (CME) meeting on Saturday to try to settle positions and sort out holdings (Wall Street Journal 1987d).

2.2 Monday, October 19, 1987

There was substantial selling pressure on the NYSE at the open on Monday with a large imbalance in the number of sell orders relative to buy orders (SEC Report 1988, p. 2-13). In this situation, many specialists did not open for trading during the first hour.[11] The SEC noted "by 10:00, 95 S&P stocks, representing 30% of the index value, were still not open" (1988, p. 2-13); the Wall Street Journal indicated that 11 of the 30 stocks in the Dow Jones Industrial Average opened late (1987e). The values of stock market indicies are calculated using the most recent price quotes for the underlying stocks. With stocks not trading, some of the quotes used to construct market indexes were stale, so the values of these indexes did not decline as much as they might have otherwise (SEC Report 1988, p. 2-13). By contrast, the futures market opened on time with heavy selling. With stale quotes in the cash market and declining prices in the futures market, a gap was created between the value of stock indexes in the cash market and in the futures market (Chicago Mercantile Exchange, Committee of Inquiry 1987, pp. 18-29). Index arbitrage traders reportedly sought to take advantage of this gap by entering sell-at-market orders on the NYSE. When stocks finally opened, prices gapped down and the index arbitragers discovered they had sold stocks considerably below what they had been expecting and tried to cover themselves by buying in the futures market. This activity precipitated a temporary rebound in prices, visible in Figure 2, but added to the confusion (Brady Report 1988, p. 30).

As stocks opened notably lower, portfolio insurers' models prompted them to resume sales. These institutions sold in both the cash and futures markets rather than just in the futures market as was typically the practice (SEC Report 1988, pp. 2-15—2-16). Sales by these and other institutions overwhelmed the rally. Significant selling continued throughout the remainder of the day

---

sell orders on behalf of customers on Monday morning and tried to pre-empt these sales.

[11]NYSE regulations allowed specialists to delay opening the stock for trading or suspend trading during the day with the permission of a floor official if the specialist believed that amount of buying or selling needed to resolve an order imbalance exceeded his obligation to provide an orderly market.

8

with equity prices declining steeply during the last hour and a half of trading. The Dow Jones Industrial Average, S&P 500, and Wilshire 5000 declined between 18 and 23 percent on the day amid deteriorating trading conditions (Brady Report 1988, Study III, p. 21). The S&P 500 futures contract declined 29 percent (SEC Report 1988, p. 2-12).

In comments following a speech, the SEC Chairman reportedly said that "there is some point, and I don't know what point that is, that I would be interested in talking to the New York Stock Exchange about a temporary, very temporary, halt in trading" (Wall Street Journal 1987f). This news broke shortly after 1:00 and started rumors in futures exchanges that the NYSE would be closed, prompting further sales as traders reportedly worried that a market close would lock them into their existing positions (Wall Street Journal 1987f).[12]

The record trading volume on Oct. 19 overwhelmed many systems. On the NYSE, for example, trade executions were reported more than an hour late, which reportedly caused confusion among traders. Investors did not know whether limit orders had been executed or whether new limits needed to be set (Brady Report 1988, Study III, p. 21).

Selling on Monday was reportedly highly concentrated. The top ten sellers accounted for 50 percent of non-market-maker volume in the futures market (Brady Report 1988, p. 36); many of these institutions were providers of portfolio insurance. One large institution started selling large blocks of stock around 10:00 in the morning and sold thirteen installments of just under $100 million each for a total of $1.1 billion during the day.

Many of the NYSE specialists reportedly tried to lean against the wind and support their stocks (though others apparently did not). The SEC reported that many specialists were heavy buyers early on Monday (SEC Report 1988, p. 4-9). However, as prices fell and the position of many specialists deteriorated, they started to lose the ability to continue to defend the stocks they

---

[12]In later Congressional testimony, the SEC Chairman stated that he had been misinterpreted. Chairman Ruder reported that in his comments he had noted that he had been in contact with the president of the NYSE prior to his speech and responded to a question regarding how one could respond to a volatile market, with a previously used statement that "Well, one of the things one might do is to have a temporary trading halt, a very, very temporary trading halt" (Ruder 1987, p. 69). The Chairman indicated that his statements about being in contact with the president of the NYSE and about a possible trading halt had not been linked in his comments but were in the press report.

9

were assigned (Brady Report 1988, Study VI, p. 42).

2.3   Tuesday, October 20, 1987

Before the opening of financial markets on Tuesday, the Federal Reserve issued a short statement that said:

> The Federal Reserve, consistent with its responsibilities as the Nation's central bank, affirmed today its readiness to serve as a source of liquidity to support the economic and financial system.

This statement reportedly contributed significantly toward supporting market sentiment (Murray 1987b). Perhaps spurred by this event, and despite precipitous declines in foreign stock markets overnight, the NYSE rebounded at the open (Brady Report 1988, p. 36-40).

Still, trading on Tuesday continued to be significantly impaired. Over the course of the day, about seven percent of stocks, including some of the most active, reportedly were closed for trading by the specialists as order imbalances made maintaining orderly markets difficult (Brady Report 1988, p. 45). Prior to the start of trading, the NYSE moved to prevent index arbitrage program traders from using the DOT system to execute trades, which may have affected the depth of the market.

Before it opens, the CME clearinghouse collects margin payments from members to cover losses that occurred the previous day on their open positions. (Margins will be discussed in some detail below.) Margin payments are then made to members for open positions in which the value improved the previous day. Typically these payments are completed by noon. On October 20, two CME clearinghouse members had not received margin payments due to them by noon, which started rumors about the solvency of the CME and its ability to make these payments. These rumors proved unfounded but nevertheless reportedly deterred some investors from trading on the CME (Brady Report 1988, p. 40). Bid-ask spreads widened, and trading was characterized as disorderly (Brady Report Study VI, pp. 64-65).

10

The typical program trading patterns were broken up. Portfolio insurers were active sellers in the futures market and pushed down prices there. Usually, index arbitragers would use this as an opportunity to buy in the futures market and sell in the cash market, which would mitigate pressure in the futures market. However, index arbitrage traders were not active, due, in part, to the NYSE's restrictions regarding use of the DOT system. This unusual pattern served to partly decouple prices in the futures and cash markets (Brady Report 1988, Study III, pp. 22-26).

With the number of trading halts for individual stocks on the NYSE and the possibility that the exchange might close, trading of many stock-index derivative products was suspended on the Chicago Board Options Exchange (CBOE) at 11:45 am and on the CME at 12:15 pm (SEC Report 1988, pp. 2-20—2-21).[13] These closures completed the de-linkage between the futures and cash markets and stocks on the NYSE began to rebound. The rise in the market was attributed in part to the removal of a "billboard," effect as the futures quotes had continually suggested that futures market participants expected the cash market to decline, and to a further reduction in selling associated with portfolio insurance (Brady Report 1988, p. 40; SEC Report 1988, p. 2-24). However, the stock market declined again once the futures markets re-opened just after 1:00 pm.

Later in the afternoon, there was a sustained rise in financial markets as corporations announced stock buyback programs to support demand for their stocks (Brady Report 1988, p. 41). Corporations had started announcing these programs Monday afternoon, but it was not until partway through Tuesday that a critical mass had formed.

---

[13]The SEC reports that the NYSE informed the commission that it was considering closing the exchange (SEC Report 1988, p. 2-20). CME Executive Committee Chairman Melamed also recalls that NYSE officials indicated to him that they might close the NYSE (Melamed and Tamakin 1996, Chapter 31).

LESSON PLAN 3B

Essential Question

How can you be a successful participant in the stock market?

Vocabulary

The following vocabulary words are important concepts for the content in this lesson:
- Bubble market
- Crash
- Insider trading
- Security and Exchange Commission

Suggested Reading Resources

Primary Source Document:
"A Brief History of the 1987 Stock Market Crash," by Mark Carlson. This document is included before the lesson in an annotated form with vocabulary underlined and some important passages for close reading highlighted; it is available online at www.teachingthroughgames.com for printing.

Mini Reading Lesson

While you are reading the available text material or the suggested reading resources, attempt to answer the following question: What happens during a bubble market and how can investors protect themselves? Introduce the vocabulary words above. They can be introduced even if they are not in the specific reading you have chosen.

GUIDED PRACTICE

Have students preview any headings and subheadings in the reading they have been asked to do. Have students read the selections.

Read and Discuss

Have students reread each section of the text and discuss the following:
- What is a bubble market?
- Why do bubble markets happen?
- How does the red stock in Panic on Wall Street resemble a bubble market?
- Is a crash always the inevitable outcome of bubble markets? Are there other factors that can cause a stock market crash?
- What role do insider information and other stock trading irregularities play in the market?

MODEL

Introduce the role of the Security and Exchange Commission in regulating the stock market and why such regulation is needed. The idea of regulating stock markets is not new; even medieval markets had laws against short sales and other shady practices. One of the most dangerous occurrences in a stock market is a bubble market, where stocks rapidly rise beyond reasonable levels. To simulate a bubble market within Panic on Wall Street, you can manipulate the cost track for the red stock. In a bubble market, costs keep rising, so remove the upper limit of 70 and let the cost keep going up on each roll. To further emphasize the inflation of the bubble, ignore any negative results. Instead, of dropping, the price simply remains steady for the round. Each round roll a regular six-sided die. If you roll a six, the market crashes and the red stock becomes worthless. Discuss what happened.

INDEPENDENT PRACTICE

Have students play the full game following the regular rules and all of the inherent chaos of those rules. This will be a noisy experience! Be prepared for yelling as investors and managers try to negotiate within an open call market. Everyone will be talking at once. Deals will be made, broken, misheard, and more. That is the nature of open call trading. To prepare students, you might show a video of the NYMEX, the New York Mercantile Exchange, where open call trading still happens. Quieter or more reserved students might want to think about strategies for being successful before they start playing.

If possible, the teacher should video record the game being played for later review. Were deals missed? How did investors and traders interact during the rounds? Were some students unable to adapt to the chaos of open call trading? Have students watch the video and then write a short response to what they saw.

Writing Activities

Remind students of the vocabulary introduced for their reading and ask them to attempt to include that vocabulary in appropriate ways in the writing activities they do.

Narrative: Write a scene for a movie script that takes place on an open call trading floor. What scenery will be needed? What will extras be doing? Write the dialog for three main characters: two investors and a business manager.

Inform or Explain: Explain why open call trading floors are not used as much today as in the past.

Express an Opinion: Should insider trading be illegal or not?

SHARING/REFLECTION

Have individuals or groups share and discuss their work with the class.

ASSESSMENT

Collect completed formative assessment (activity for model section) and writing activities and review. For the reflection on the game play video, accept any reasonable answers for which support is provided from the video. In the narrative, the background information should depict a noisy, chaotic scene with the main characters engaging in negotiations. The main reasons for the decline in open call trading are the computers that are now running most transactions faster than humans can follow. Additional research may be required for this piece. The ethical considerations in the opinion piece may go either direction, but a sophisticated answer will reflect that the stock market works as an investment tool only if the element of chance is shared by all involved.

EXTENSION ACTIVITIES

Further Research: What happened during the technology stock bubble market of the early 2000s?

Further Research: Explore the role of computers and computer programs in micro transactions within modern stock markets. With trades happening faster than humans can follow, computer programs can (and have) caused mini bubbles and crashes that take place in mere seconds as programs run wild.

LESSON 4:
PUTTING IT TOGETHER
IN CHICAGO EXPRESS

Building on the ideas introduced in the last three chapters, it is now time to turn students loose to run a business. In Chicago Express (Queen Games, 2007), players take on the role of investors buying shares in and helping to run different train companies. To be successful, students will have to budget their money, balance spending and saving, assess risk, and calculate return on investment.

FINANCIAL LITERACY INFORMATION

HISTORICAL CONTEXT

Chicago Express is an exemplar of a whole genre of tabletop games built around trains. The game provides a simplified experience that still manages to capture many of the concepts found in the larger games. The genre is popular not only because of the trains involved, but also because of the detailed business and investing simulations embedded in the games. Historically, the 1800s were an amazing period of rapid development and expansion in the United States. It began in the first part of the century with a bold proposal to build a canal from the Hudson River at Albany, New York, to Lake Erie at Buffalo, New York. When the Erie Canal opened in 1825, it quickly reduced the cost of shipping goods between New York City and Buffalo from about $100 a ton to about $4 a ton.[4] More importantly, Buffalo's location on the eastern end of Lake Erie provided uninterrupted access to the Midwest. The abundant food from the prairies was now accessible for the growing cities on the Atlantic seaboard. Canal travel was slow, though, and the growing economic engine in New York City wanted a faster link to the resources of the Midwest and the newly acquired lands in the West ceded by Mexico in 1848 at the end of the Mexican-American War.

The answer was railroads. In 1850, there was only one railroad servicing Chicago, Illinois. By 1852 there were five railroads; by 1856 that number had doubled. The population in Chicago more than tripled during the 1850s from 30,000 at the start of the decade to over 109,000 by the end of it.[5] Competition was fierce, and the first railroads that were about to establish a nonstop connection from the East Coast to Chicago enjoyed great success. The first New York to Chicago railroad was finished in January 1853 on what would become the New York Central Railroad. In 1857 the Pennsylvania Railroad established a direct connection between Chicago and Philadelphia; in 1874 the Baltimore and Ohio Railroad reached Chicago as well. The last major railroad represented in Chicago Express, the Chesapeake & Ohio Railroad, never built a direct track, but through acquisitions of other railroads had connected Virginia to Chicago by the late 1880s.

MAXIMIZING SHAREHOLDER VALUE

The shareholders who owned stock in the railroad companies that made it to Chicago profited greatly. In the game, this is represented by a large increase in the value of the stock and a bonus dividend payout. Dividends are the money paid out from profits by a company to shareholders. Even though the process is built into the rules for Chicago Express as part of the simplification, companies don't always pay out dividends. In more detailed railroad games, company presidents have to decide whether to pay out dividends or to reinvest profits in the company. Reinvesting profits in the company may be necessary to maintain tracks or buy new locomotives, but in these games companies are punished for not paying dividends with a sharp decline in stock value. This representation is not historically accurate. Henry Ford was famous for reinvesting profits back into the company to improve the cars produced and pay better wages. As games designed today, though, the economic system is heavily influenced by the modern adherence to the concept of maximizing shareholder value.

In a 2013 article about IBM, the *Washington Post* referred to a "deep-seated belief that took hold in corporate America a few decades ago and has come to define today's economy—that a company's primary purpose is to maximize shareholder value."[6] The business model driving most of the multinational corporations that dominate the market today is therefore to maximize shareholder value. Not to make things or solve problems, but rather to do what it takes to increase the price of the stock and thereby enhance shareholder value. The products produced and services delivered are simply helpful byproducts of the quest for higher stock prices.

The belief that shareholders come first is not codified by statute. Rather, it was introduced by a handful of free-market academics in the 1970s and then picked up by business leaders and the media until it became an oft-repeated mantra in the corporate world. Together with new competition overseas, the pressure to respond to the short-term demands of Wall Street has paved the way for an economy in which companies are increasingly disconnected from the state of the nation, laying off workers in huge waves, keeping average wages low and threatening to move operations abroad in the face of regulations and taxes.[7]

In his 1999 novel *Cryptonomicon*, science fiction author Neal Stephenson satirized the dedication to shareholder value:

> MISSION: At [name of company] it is our conviction that [to do the stuff we want to do] and to increase shareholder value are not merely complementary activities—they are inextricably linked. PURPOSE: To increase shareholder value by [doing stuff].[8]

This is only just slightly over-the-top. As economist Milton Friedman famously opined in a 1970 piece in the *New York Times*, the only social responsibility of a business is to increase its profits.[9] We as consumers are partially complicit in this. The push to lower prices on clothing and other consumer goods has led to sweatshops and other serious problems with overseas working conditions. When the mission and purpose of a company is to increase shareholder value, then abusing workers in a foreign sweatshop to lower costs and increase profits becomes a necessity. As Stephenson advances the plot of his novel, the threat of shareholder lawsuits is a constant worry for the characters.

COMPETITION VS. COOPERATION

Chicago Express provides an opportunity for players to avoid the hyper-competitive environment that drives the focus on shareholder value. In the game, you are not playing as one of the companies, but rather as a general investor who can buy stock in any (or even all) of the companies. You then guide the development of the companies in which you are invested by having them build track and improve stations. When two players have an equal number of shares in a company, it is in their mutual best interest to have that company succeed. If one player has more stock than any others in the company, however, all bets are off. This is especially true for the Pennsylvania Railroad Company, the red stock. With only three shares of stock available, it is quite probable that they will not be evenly distributed. The company is in a precarious position, though, as it also has the smallest number of train figures for building track to Chicago; there are only two more trains available than are needed for the shortest route. That makes it very easy for a minority shareholder to sabotage the company and prevent it from reaching Chicago.

In the last few years a new type of corporate organization has been codified in the laws of sixteen states and Washington, D.C., allowing companies that focus on public good as opposed to just shareholder value. In 2010, Maryland became the first state to pass a law creating benefit corporations or B-corporations. These are for-profit companies that have established social, environmental, or other public-good goals beyond just enhancing shareholder value. This protects the company from lawsuits about failing to maximize shareholder value, but it isn't a free pass. "Whereas a regular business can abandon altruistic policies when times get tough," a *New Yorker* article in 2014 notes, "a benefit corporation can't. Shareholders can sue its directors for not carrying out the company's social mission, just as they can sue directors of traditional companies for violating their fiduciary duty."[10] B-corporations provide legal protection for a new generation of companies that want to be successful and profitable, but not at the expense of the world and their workers. How might Chicago Express or other economic games be different if there were B-corporations in the rules?

LESSON PLAN 4A

ESSENTIAL QUESTION

How do competition and cooperation influence the business marketplace?

VOCABULARY

The following vocabulary words are important concepts for the content in this lesson:

- Competition
- Cooperation
- Shareholder value
- Dividend

GUIDED PRACTICE

Introduce the vocabulary words above and discuss what the students have learned in this lesson and in prior lessons about financial literacy. Discuss the following:

- Thinking about the history of railroad companies, why did companies start to cooperate on shared tracks?
- Why did people invest in railroad companies?
- Think about modern comparisons for shared infrastructure and cooperation such as power companies selling electricity over a common grid or websites sending information across a shared network. How do competition and cooperation work in these scenarios and how is it related to railroad companies of the past?

MODEL

Make sure that students understand that they are investors, not managers or owners of a company. Because this is a capstone game for financial literacy and more complex than the other games played, in this lesson the students, in small groups, will be asked to explore the game board, pieces, and rules of play for the game.

INDEPENDENT PRACTICE

After a review of the rules of play and game components, the students, in their small groups, will need to relate the game play to what they have experienced in the previous financial literacy games. While this action is independent practice, the teacher will need to listen to the small group dialogues and facilitate students' thinking about relationships to earlier concepts and the play of this game. At the end of the review time, each group will be asked to submit a list of ten concepts from other games and how they each relate to playing Chicago Express.

Writing Activities: Remind students of the vocabulary introduced for their reading and ask them to attempt to include that vocabulary in appropriate ways in the writing activities they do.
Inform or Explain: Expand on some costs and opportunities of investing in a railroad expansion.

SHARING/REFLECTION

Have individuals or groups share and discuss their work with the class. Keep a compiled list of the points made, summarizing and linking ideas as necessary, to have a complete class list of concepts.

ASSESSMENT

Collect completed formative assessment (activity for model section) and writing activities and review. The small group list should have concepts from the previous financial literacy games and clear links to Chicago Express. Look for links such as the auction components found in High Society, the risk assessment and ROI analysis from Can't Stop, and the stock market evaluations from Panic on Wall Street. Sophisticated analysis might also include the need for pre-budgeting to determine reasonable stock prices to provide a company with enough funds to reach Chicago.

EXTENSION ACTIVITIES

Further Research: How is Kickstarter similar to and different from being an investor in a company?

LESSON PLAN 4B

ESSENTIAL QUESTION

How is Chicago Express a good example of financial literacy concepts put in practice?

VOCABULARY

Because this is a capstone game for financial literacy and the last lesson of the book, no new vocabulary is introduced. The focus is on playing the larger game using prior knowledge gained through the previous lessons.

MODEL

The teacher will review the components and the rules for Chicago Express. Refer back to the list of similarities developed in the prior lesson to draw upon background knowledge about auctions, risk assessment, ROI evaluation, and stock market interactions.

INDEPENDENT PRACTICE

Have students play the full game of Chicago Express using the regular rules. The game supports up to five players. Playing for the first time may take longer than a single class period. The goal of this experience is to have students think critically about how all of the different aspects of financial literacy explored in the other games combine in Chicago Express. While the object of the game is to have the most money in hand at the end of the game through engaging in profitable stock investments, the educational objective is to have students demonstrate the application of financial literacy concepts. During game play, pause for meta-review of the game experience. After the initial auction, for example, have groups discuss and share with the class as a whole how their auction went. Did some groups get into a bidding war? Did some players have a plan for budgeting their money to allow auction purchases during the first round of the game? Encourage groups to continue pausing for discussions after each dividend payout.

At the end of the game, have students complete the Financial Literacy Concept sheet located in the appendix and available online at www.teachingthroughgames.com for printing. The sheet asks students to reflect on how the identified financial literacy concepts were used while playing Chicago Express.

Writing Activities

Express an Opinion: List the three most important concepts you have gained from playing these games about financial literacy. Provide specific examples of how your new understandings might be used in your life.

Sharing/Reflection

Have individuals or groups share and discuss their reactions to playing Chicago Express with the class.

Assessment

Assessment in this case will occur through observation of students playing the game. The Financial Literacy Concepts sheet should correctly identify relationships between Chicago Express and prior learning. The opinion piece should demonstrate a broad understanding of the different concepts addressed throughout the book.

EXTENSION ACTIVITIES

Further Research: Explore the recent creation of benefit corporations. How might these for-profit companies that are also focused on the public good change business?

APPENDIX 1
CURRICULUM ALIGNMENTS

COMMON CORE LEARNING STANDARDS

The following concepts from the Common Core State Standards are addressed in this unit:

READING INFORMATIONAL TEXTS RELATED TO GRADE 9-12 STANDARDS

- CCSS.ELA-LITERACY.RI.9-10.1
  Cite strong and thorough textual evidence to support analysis of what the text says explicitly as well as inferences drawn from the text.
- CCSS.ELA-LITERACY.RI.9-10.5
  Analyze in detail how an author's ideas or claims are developed and refined by particular sentences, paragraphs, or larger portions of a text (e.g., a section or chapter).
- CCSS.ELA-LITERACY.RI.11-12.1
  Cite strong and thorough textual evidence to support analysis of what the text says explicitly as well as inferences drawn from the text, including determining where the text leaves matters uncertain.
- CCSS.ELA-LITERACY.RI.11-12.7
  Integrate and evaluate multiple sources of information presented in different media or formats (e.g., visually, quantitatively) as well as in words in order to address a question or solve a problem.

WRITING STANDARDS RELATED TO GRADE 9-12 STANDARDS

- CCSS.ELA-LITERACY.W.9-10.1 and

CCSS.ELA-LITERACY.W.11-12.1
Write arguments to support claims in an analysis of substantive topics or texts, using valid reasoning and relevant and sufficient evidence.

- CCSS.ELA-LITERACY.W.9-10.2 and
CCSS.ELA-LITERACY.W.11-12.2
Write informative/explanatory texts to examine and convey complex ideas, concepts, and information clearly and accurately through the effective selection, organization, and analysis of content.

- CCSS.ELA-LITERACY.W.9-10.3 and
CCSS.ELA-LITERACY.W.11-12.3
Write narratives to develop real or imagined experiences or events using effective technique, well-chosen details, and well-structured event sequences.

- CCSS.ELA-LITERACY.W.9-10.6
Use technology, including the Internet, to produce, publish, and update individual or shared writing products, taking advantage of technology's capacity to link to other information and to display information flexibly and dynamically.

- CCSS.ELA-LITERACY.W.9-10.7 and
CCSS.ELA-LITERACY.W.11-12.7
Conduct short as well as more sustained research projects to answer a question (including a self-generated question) or solve a problem; narrow or broaden the inquiry when appropriate; synthesize multiple sources on the subject, demonstrating understanding of the subject under investigation.

- CCSS.ELA-LITERACY.W.9-10.8
Gather relevant information from multiple authoritative print and digital sources, using advanced searches effectively; assess the usefulness of each source in answering the research question; integrate information into the text selectively to maintain the flow of ideas, avoiding plagiarism and following a standard format for citation.

- CCSS.ELA-LITERACY.W.11-12.8

Gather relevant information from multiple authoritative print and digital sources, using advanced searches effectively; assess the strengths and limitations of each source in terms of the task, purpose, and audience; integrate information into the text selectively to maintain the flow of ideas, avoiding plagiarism and overreliance on any one source and following a standard format for citation.

- CCSS.ELA-LITERACY.W.9-10.9 and CCSS.ELA-LITERACY.W.11-12.9
  Draw evidence from literary or informational texts to support analysis, reflection, and research.

FINANCIAL LITERACY STANDARDS RELATED TO GRADE 9-12 STANDARDS

Standards for Financial literacy from:
  http://www.councilforeconed.org/wp/wp-content/uploads/2013/02/national-standards-for-financial-literacy.pdf

Buying Goods and Services
Students will understand that:
People cannot buy or make all the goods and services they want; as a result, people choose to buy some goods and services and not buy others. People can improve their economic well-being by making informed spending decisions, which entails collecting information, planning, and budgeting.

Protecting and Insuring
Students will understand that:
People make choices to protect themselves from the financial risk of lost income, assets, health, or identity. They can choose to accept risk, reduce risk, or transfer the risk to others. Insurance allows people to transfer risk by paying a fee now to avoid the possibility of a larger loss later. The price of insurance is influenced by an individual's behavior.

Saving
Students will understand that:

Saving is the part of income that people choose to set aside for future uses. People save for different reasons during the course of their lives. People make different choices about how they save and how much they save. Time, interest rates, and inflation affect the value of savings.

Using credit
Students will understand that:

Credit allows people to purchase goods and services that they can use today and pay for in the future with interest. People choose among different credit options that have different costs. Lenders approve or deny applications for loans based on an evaluation of the borrower's past credit history and expected ability to pay in the future. Higher-risk borrowers are charged higher interest rates; lower-risk borrowers are charged lower interest rates.

Financial Investing
Students will understand that:

Financial investment is the purchase of financial assets to increase income or wealth in the future. Investors must choose among investments that have different risks and expected rates of return. Investments with higher expected rates of return tend to have greater risk. Diversification of investment among a number of choices can lower investment risk.

APPENDIX 2

DATA GATHERING SHEETS

To access supplementary materials, go to http://www.teachingthrough-games.com. Then enter the code word **spendwell** in order to be directed to the following worksheets:

Important Details Worksheet

TEACHING THROUGH GAMES
TEACHING FINANCIAL LITERACY THROUGH PLAY

	Important Detail	Reason Chosen
1		
2		
3		
4		
5		
6		
7		
8		
9		
10		

ABOUT THE AUTHORS

Christopher Harris, Editorial Director   chris@playplaylearn.com Chris is the director of a School Library System in western New York that has provided a curriculum aligned board game library to member school districts since 2007. His current position as a certified school administrator, along with his background as a teacher, technology coordinator, and school librarian have provided Chris with many different perspectives on gaming and learning. Being able to speak with fellow administrators including principals and curriculum directors about the value of board games as a part of teaching and learning has been key to the success of the game library he founded as part of the Genesee Valley Educational Partnership School Library System in 2007. Chris was a member of the National Expert Panel for the American Library Association Gaming and Libraries grant in 2007-2008 and has continued to present nationally on gaming in schools and libraries as well as other school, technology and library topics. He writes a monthly column in School Library Journal called "The Next Big Thing" and co-authored *Libraries Got Game: Aligned Learning through Modern Board Games* (ALA Editions, 2010) with Brian Mayer.

Dr. Patricia Harris, Curriculum & Instruction   pat@playplaylearn. com After working more than 10 years in public schools both rural and urban and spending 8 years at an engineering school teaching social sciences, communication skills, and technology, Dr. Patricia Harris spent the last years of her career as head of an elementary education program, technology coordinator for the education department, and educational consultant for a physicians assistant graduate program. Her research and practical focus in education has been working with teachers at all grade levels, including working with an elementary teacher to co-teach a clinical class for several years, to build pedagogical strength. Dr. Harris's experience with social studies and science instructional methodology helps inform the curriculum alignment and classroom use scenarios presented here.

NOTES

NOTES